# Heaven Upon Earth

*The Countryside Remembered*

# Heaven Upon Earth

## *The Countryside Remembered*

Tom Quinn

*Photographs by John Tarlton*

SWAN·HILL
PRESS

For Pam Tarlton

Text copyright © 2005 Tom Quinn
Photographs copyright © 2005 Estate of John Tarlton

First published in the UK in 2005
by Swan Hill Press, an imprint of Quiller Publishing Ltd

**British Library Cataloguing-in-Publication Data**
   A catalogue record for this book
   is available from the British Library

ISBN 1 904057 67 5

Printed in China

**Swan Hill Press**
An imprint of Quiller Publishing Ltd
Wykey House, Wykey, Shrewsbury, SY4 1JA
Tel: 01939 261616 Fax: 01939 261606
E-mail: info@quillerbooks.com
Website: www.swanhillbooks.com

# Contents

1. Introduction
7

2. The Farming Year
13

3. Country Characters
63

4. House and Garden
71

5. Country Crafts
89

6. Sports and Pastimes
113

*A rare photograph showing the photographer John Tarlton at work – he was a perfectionist who believed in getting the right position for every shot!*

# 1.
# INTRODUCTION

Until the Second World War – and even, in some areas, until the late 1950s and early 1960s – the British countryside had changed little over the centuries. Horses had replaced oxen it is true and the great fields divided into strips had gone, but the countryside was still a place where mechanisation had made only minor inroads.

Before the war steady pace of rural life was largely dictated by the horse; animals were still occasionally driven to market along the ancient drovers' roads and tiny fields surrounded by well-grown hedges dominated much of the landscape. The countryside was also a much more densely populated place than it is today; a lowland farmer might employ a shepherd, a team of horsemen and their assistants, a cowman, milkmaids and odd-job men. All had their tied cottages and though they often lived at or beneath the poverty line, they had sufficient income to fuel a local economy of shops, pubs, blacksmiths, wheelwrights and farriers that has all but disappeared.

It was common throughout England to meet old men and women who had never been outside their county, let alone to London or abroad. One elderly farmer interviewed in 1980 recalled that his father and four uncles lived all their lives in Norfolk without ever even travelling the thirty miles to Norwich.

It was the Second World War that accelerated a process of change in the countryside which had begun during the Great War. Change had to come because, at a time of national crisis, it was essential that farmers should use the latest chemicals and technology in order to produce the maximum amount of food. After that there was no going back.

With the coming of the mass-produced motor car, the introduction of tractors and combine harvesters and the development of chemical fertilisers, the last great movement from the land to the towns and cities began.

The heavy horses that had powered the farming world for so long began to disappear along with most of the farmworkers' jobs, and, by the 1960s, many villages were rapidly changing into mere dormitories for the towns. Men who might once have worked on the land now drove away from the village each day to work in factories and offices.

The photographer John Tarlton recorded this countryside, its inhabitants, its villages and farms just as they were about to change forever. The bulk of his pictures was taken from the late 1940s to the early 1960s and they record a world that was already disappearing fast. He photographed pubs with open fires, stone floors and simple wooden benches where old men played dominoes, and juke boxes and gambling machines were unknown; he recorded the overgrown lanes where farm horses walked slowly home in the evening and where cars were only occasionally seen; he tracked down traditional gypsies who still travelled in brightly covered carts; and he sought out wheelwrights and farriers, shepherds and horsemen, basketmakers and harness men before they vanished forever.

This book celebrates John Tarlton's work and through it the last years of what was essentially a pre-industrial countryside; a countryside we will never see again.

7

OPPOSITE: *The carter makes his way home near Fairstead in Essex.*

*Wheelright at Bratton. Fred Davis smoothing the face of the new elm felloes which he has fitted to a wagon wheel.* 9

John Tarlton, whose work is celebrated in this book, was born in Essex in 1914. His father encouraged his interest in photography and by the time he enlisted in the RAF in 1939 he was hooked. He joined the RAF photographic unit, serving in Canada and the Far East. After the war he started his own photographic business in Fairstead in Essex and it was here that he began to record the countryside about him. John loved the English countryside and was saddened to see the decline of the village and the traditions and traditional landscape he had known as a boy disappearing under the onslaught of the motorcar and farm mechanisation.

All this happened during the 1950s and 60s when he did some of his best work. He photographed the tiny village shops, the few still unmade roads, the great heavy horses and carts, the meadows and byways. He took photographs of the last of the traditional shepherds and ploughmen, of hedgerows being laid, and of the great open skies of Essex, the county he had loved and known since he was a boy.

But he also travelled to the West Country, to Hampshire, Gloucestershire, Wales and Scotland; and for the last three decades of his life he lived by the sea in Christchurch, Hampshire.

10   *Pre-tractor era. Horsemen picking up the traces at sunrise before beginning a day's ploughing on an Essex farm.*

*The ford over the River Chelmer at Great Easton, near Dunmow. Essex.* 11

From the 1950s right up to 1980, the year of his death, and despite all the changes he had seen in his lifetime, he continued to photograph country people, farms and farmworkers, landscapes and animals. In all the thousands of pictures he took his eye was invariably drawn to scenes that summed up a special moment or which moved him deeply. He was fascinated by landscape and the changes of the seasons, but he also delighted in the humble tasks of the farming year. It was the broad sweep of his interest that made – and makes – his work so special.

However, John was also a great technician who believed that the skill of the darkroom had much to contribute to the overall success of a particular image. Wherever his pictures were kept on file it was a truism among researchers and editors that you could never mistake a John Tarlton print for the work of any other photographer. There was never any need to check the credit on the back of the picture: the fact that it was by John was always obvious even to the greenest newcomer. And the reason? Simply that John used his extraordinary darkroom skills to create a unique series of finished prints. Like many great photographers he believed that the full potential of each photograph would be lost if one simply assumed that a negative could be routinely processed.

John Tarlton was a self-effacing man and, ironically, this was most obvious when it came to photography – he was instantly inclined to run a mile if it looked as if anyone might point a camera at him!

# 2.
# THE FARMING YEAR

*The old ploughman – his furrow is as straight as a die. Hurn, Hampshire.*

The farming year has always dominated the countryside. In winter, ploughing occupied thousands of farmworkers in the laborious business of preparing the soil at the rate, on average, of just one acre a day. There was also general repair work to be done about the farm, as well as hedge-laying and ditch-clearing, the latter often done by itinerant labourers who earned a pittance for back-breaking work and who slept rough. Most farms were still mixed and cattle, pigs and sheep all needed feeding and looking after.

In an interview in 1980, Aubrey Charman, whose family had farmed in Kent since the mid 1700s, recalled the details of working with horses on the farm where his family had lived for almost two centuries.

'Seven cart-horses did everything here until the late 1950s. I'd have been about ten when I first remember leading them. Always slowly, always at a walk. A cart-horse never runs or trots, but they'll do three miles an hour and the smallest boy can lead and stop them when they're trained.

'Ours were trained by the farmworkers – we had eight farmworkers normally and two pupils who would generally have been eighteen or perhaps nineteen. We had farm cottages then too. They've gone now but each man had a cottage with the job in the early days and we never turfed them out when they retired. They stayed till they died or went into a home.

'Winters were generally much worse when I was young and summers better than now – Father had always finished the harvest by the time we get started these days. We still have the dates the harvest finished carved on our granary wall and they go back more than one hundred years.'

Records suggest that winters were indeed generally much harsher in the first half of the twentieth century and a harsh winter made everything more difficult, whether ploughing or simply getting about. Aubrey had particularly distinct memories of the terrible winter of 1963 when, of necessity, there was a return to the old ways.

'The traffic came to a halt in this part of Kent so deep were the roads and lanes in snow. The farm milk couldn't be collected and after three days – because, of course, the cows had still to be milked – all the farm churns were full.

'With sixteen full churns my wife and I toured every street in Southwater in a horse and cart. I rang a big bell and shouted "Milk!" at the top of my voice. People came out and stopped us and my wife filled their cans and jugs as required. As they hadn't had a delivery for three days they were more than happy.'

Cart-horses and plough horses would only work well if they were well looked after. They had special needs, too, which explains at least partly why so many farms had small ponds in or near the farmyard. Aubrey Charman again:

'Our pond was built about a hundred years ago chiefly for washing the farm horses' legs. That's why it's got a solid stone bottom. When they're ploughing, heavy horses get their legs badly caked with mud – particularly it gathers on the long hair above the hoofs. If the mud isn't cleaned off they get a terrible affliction we called farcy. So every evening at ploughing time the horses would be tied nose to tail and led to the pond. Then they'd be driven round in it for a few minutes until all the mud on their legs had washed off. The youngest ploughman normally rode the first horse round and round to make it go and the others followed. We did this right through the ploughing time until we got our first tractors.'

Through winter and summer some things didn't change. Milking and the tasks associated with it, for example, were a year-round responsibility. For Aubrey domestic servants were actually far more like co-workers in the farm business.

'We had a housemaid and a dairymaid, who would help milk the cows and clean the dairy utensils. Every day two large pails of milk were put through the separator to separate the cream from the skim milk. The skim milk was fed to the calves until they were eight weeks old. All female calves were kept to go into the dairy herd when they were mature at about three years old.'

For the small farmer, times could be very hard indeed, but for the farm worker – even the skilled ploughman – life was even tougher, particularly between the wars, as Norfolk ploughman William Constance recalled.

William, who was interviewed aged ninety-two, in the mid-1980s, remembered how the horses were always fed before the men and how ploughing varied according to the land. It was a world apart from the modern world of social security and redundancy pay.

'I worked at Rose Farm and when the owner died I was out of a job. You just moved then in those circumstances. You got up and left; no dole, no social

*Hoar frost on the hedgerow. Essex.* 15

*North
Devon lane,
evening,
near
Batworthy.*

security, no redundancy money. But by then I was a pretty good ploughman so I quickly found another place. I'd learned to plough two horses side by side which is the way we did it in Norfolk and we used a two-furrow plough.

'At the ploughing time we were up at six o'clock every day which is hard on a young boy, but we knew nothing else and got used to it I suppose. At six then, we fed the horses first – on chaff and corn ground up and mashed together. That was in the stable, but when we turned them out we fed them hay which was put in the iron ricks for them. At night they were turned out into a walled yard which isn't done any more and I don't know why we did it then. But they were always put in the yard rather than in the field or kept in their stalls.

'I would calculate that in the Scole area of Norfolk there were roughly four horses and four men to every one hundred acres of land. That's a lot of men and horses. And you imagine those numbers going right across Norfolk and probably Suffolk too – you can imagine how many people there were in the countryside. Not like now where each farm is lucky if it has one man and everyone else gets in a car and dashes off to the nearest town to work. The countryside is empty today; empty compared to what it was when I was a young man anyway.'

*Harrowing near Great Bardfield Windmill, Essex.* 17

*The last load is carried to the farm. Old-time harvest in Essex.*

William saw ploughing as the great challenge of farm life but it was a task in which man and horse had to take account of the conditions and their own limitations.

'On light soil the horses could just walk away with it. But on heavy clay they'd be all of a tremble and winded before they were half way up a field. Often they'd stop half way and they'd be shaking and blowing. You'd have to let them rest then. It was hard work even for a great strong horse here in Norfolk. Hard work for the man, too, in all weathers, perhaps with only a sack over his shoulders to keep the rain off and miles to walk behind that plough in a day.

'On our land you'd be pushed to cover half or three-quarters of an acre in a day, and a man walked fourteen miles with his horses to plough one acre. It was hard work but there was harder.

'A good man would hardly touch the plough handles or the horses. They'd be a real team and know what they were about, with the horses turning on the headland at a word from the ploughman and he'd be as straight as a die up the field.'

Will recalled ploughing from late September until January and when the horses weren't ploughing they were used to cart things. On Will's farm barley was sold to brewers in nearby Diss or Eye. The barley was carried in what were known as cwmb sacks, each cart holding roughly thirty sacks. Thirty sacks made roughly three tons which could only be pulled by three horses and with a load like this they travelled at about three miles an hour. The horses never trotted, as Will explains.

'Trotting was just really bad for the horses. You'd get the sack for trotting them. That was a certainty if you were found out. It's easy enough to drive a great heavy wagon and three horses so long as you let the horses get on with it. I used to sit on the front of the beet wagon with the reins tied loosely on the harness – driving by mouth we called it. In other words I'd just tell the horses what to do. I never had to use the stick or the reins.

'We used old shire horses when I was young. They were fine to work with, but by the 1950s they'd been replaced by Suffolk punches. Now they really were powerful great animals, but good tempered most of them. They were also cleaner than the old shire horse which was all hair and if you didn't keep his hairy legs cleaned regularly he got all sorts of problems and went lame.

'In the field while he worked, too, the old shire could get so bogged down with mud that he almost couldn't move. We had to stop in the middle of the field to hack the mud off him to keep him going.'

But ploughing was just one part of the horses' work. Apart from carting, there was also harrowing and sowing. This was less arduous than ploughing, as was hoeing which was also done with horses. During horse-hoeing the man led the way with the horse following behind.

And crops were far more varied before farming became an industrial affair.

'The main crops in my youth were wheat, barley and oats' William remembered. 'Oats were very important because we used them for animal feed, feed for the cows, sheep and horses. We also grew beans and peas. Today, of course, the farmers grow what the European Union tells them to grow and nothing else and there's little skill in it. Plenty of chemicals, plenty of machines and that's it. Not much skill at all. And not much effort either – though I suppose that has to be a good thing.'

Farming was certainly an exhausting business before mechanisation. Farmers rarely took holidays in those days. William reckoned he'd had a total of five weeks' holiday in all his ninety-two years. Work was simply a permanent fact of life – even for the old and infirm.

'Old women were paid to pick stones from the field into heaps and these were used on the roads. The women got two bob a ton I think. They had to put them in heaps and then the farmer would collect all the stones in a cart and carry them to the road where groups of very old men, perhaps from the workhouse, were employed to break the stones into small pieces and spread them on the road.'

Keeping the roads in a half decent state was almost a year-round job because by winter there were always new potholes to fill and if they weren't filled quickly they got deeper and deeper.

On many farms spring meant lambing time – a time that relied on the skills and dedication of the shepherd if the maximum number of lambs were to survive their first few hazardous hours and days of life.

'Sometimes the weather at lambing time was very good, but it could be terrible,' says William. 'Then we used what we called lamb clothes, round hurdles designed to keep the wind off the lambs in their first few vulnerable hours. The old shepherd I learned with had a tiny hut out in the fields and we drank rum to keep out the cold.

*Cotswold shepherd at lambing time.*

*Head shepherd Jack Batchelor with a young lamb in one of the coops. Chilmark, Wiltshire.* 21

22    *Bringing lambs in from the hill by horse.*

His hut was about twelve feet square with a wooden bench at one side and a stove that he kept burning with wood continually. There was a chair where I sat while the candle threatened to go out at any moment in the draught. The shepherd lay on the hard bench. He lived there for weeks at a time – all the time the sheep were lambing – and he could never wash or anything, but no one thought that much about that then since no one had baths in their houses or even inside loos. Just a hole dug in the garden and moved when it filled up.'

The shepherd was brought food every day by someone in his family and when lambing was over he left the hut for another year. The harshness of the farmworker's life meant that even simple items like footwear and clothing had to be of the toughest quality.

Will again:

'The men always wore hob-nailed boots made of the thickest leather. If they got soaked they'd be as hard as hell the next morning when you came to put them on. And tough though they were they would generally last only a year. But we wore them every day and a man only ever had the one pair. A pair of boots might cost fifteen shillings and I reckon every working man in Norfolk wore the same sort. It wasn't until after the war that I got something different – they were lace-up rubber boots and they lasted as long as leather boots, but were more comfortable.

'We all wore waistcoats too – the men I mean – and special ploughman's trousers. These were of soft very thick cloth.'

*Harvesters at work in the late evening carting barley in August near Broomfield, Essex.*   23

Will's descriptions of some aspects of farm life have an almost eighteenth century ring to them. When he was a young man for example, summer meant cutting the hay and the corn by hand.

'We were very systematic about it. The headman would start mowing up the field first and the others would one by one fall in behind him and to the right hand side. Perhaps fifteen men would mow and if the weather was right it would all be carted loose. There would be two on top of the cart and two on the ground forking the hay up to the men on top. It had to be laid carefully in a circle on top of the cart because if you put it on any old way you wouldn't get much on. Four of us might cart ten acres in a day in this way. Then we'd take it in to the farmyard and unload it.

'Our ricks were normally ten yards by five yards – roughly the height of a twenty stave ladder and they would have thatched roofs just like a house.

'To thatch the roof you'd make up what we called a yellum of straw; you'd put six yellums in a yoke and then tie that in a bundle. Up on the stack a man would undo the yoke, which was just a bundle of straw tied with rope – and pin it to the stack with an iron clip. Bit by bit the whole thing would be pinned and covered nice and waterproof.'

Hayricks were vital because farms tended to be self-sufficient as far as possible and that sense of local sustainability was reflected in the fact that most of the farm produce tended to be sold locally, although some went to London.

'All our milk went to Diss and from there on the train to London. We took it by cart every day to the station and twice a day in summertime. When we were taking cattle to market we'd drive them along the open road into Diss – in those days there were gates everywhere along the roads so the animals couldn't wander off into people's gardens or into fields. Pigs were driven along the road just the same and we never lost any even when we walked them – as occasionally we did – to Norwich.'

The portrait painted by Will Constance echoes the memories of many other farmers, but there were regional variations. On the other side of England Reg Dobson grew up on a small remote farm in Shropshire. When he left school he was immediately plunged into the world of work, as he explains.

'I was expected to work seven days a week from six in the morning till six at night. There were 125 cows to milk by hand every day – unless you've actually done that yourself you can have no idea of the work involved.

'There were twelve of us did the milking and we did it according to a number system so that each person had his or her fair share of difficult cows – you know, cows that tried to bite you or that kicked like hell.

'If they thought they could get away with it, people would deliberately take a long time at an easy cow until they could see that another easy one was next in line to be milked. We used to put a special leather strap on the kickers to keep their legs still, but some started to kick before you even got near them.

'An old man called Punch used to carry off the pails of milk as they were filled. He wore a great wooden yoke, like you'd put on a pair of oxen, and on each side would be suspended the pail. In my first year I also had to do the sheep. They were mostly Cheviots and the devil to catch because we had no proper pens. I used to get the dog to hold them in a corner of the field and then run in and catch the one I wanted. Half the time it was a question of run in and dive at a fleeing sheep – a bit like a rugby tackle.'

In Shropshire, shearing time meant a slight improvement on the old simple hand shears – they were now crank driven.

'An old local poacher called Jim Carne used to come at shearing time. I used to turn the handle of the wheel that drove the shears – we'd come on a bit from simple hand shears – and he did the clipping. He was very good at it but it was hard work for a sixteen year old turning that thing all day.'

If you had any hope of surviving on a Shropshire farm between the wars, you had to be a shrewd dealer. Selling your produce in the days before intervention buying by the European Union was the severest test of a farmer's ability in the market place. Reg again:

'Dad was a sharp one for selling sheep. He'd buy them and get us to trim them and clean them till they looked really smart and then he'd take them straight back to market and usually get a pound or two each more than he paid for them.'

OPPOSITE: *The heart of Suffolk: a stubble field near Saxmundham with thatched ricks in the distance.*

*As the sun sinks in the west behind the old post-mill at Brill in Buckinghamshire, a farmer crosses the ridge carrying his pails on a yoke.*

*Haymaking near Terling in Essex before the Second World War. The traditional scene on a June day when the hay is dry and in fit condition for stacking.*  27

28    *Dorset. A trackway across the Downs at harvest time.*

*Open farmland and trees across the broad sweep of Dorset's Tarrant Valley.*    29

*The double Gloucester cheesemaker.*

Self-sufficiency was also important at a time when many farms were part of isolated communities and much of the three hundred gallons of milk a day the Dobsons' cows produced went to make cheese. The cheese was made on site by a cheesemaker who lived in with the family and because nothing was ever wasted, large quantities of whey – a by-product of the cheesemaking process – had to be stored and then fed to the pigs.

'It was kept in a big brick tank and then I used to take it by the bucketful to feed the pigs. I had a yoke on my shoulders which made it a bit easier, but it was incredibly hard work, particularly on your legs. And we had what would now be considered very unbalanced rations in those days for the animals – we'd prepare a great barrow full of maize germ meal and then tip it in the pigs' trough; then we'd pour the whey on top – there was an awful lot got trodden in and slopped about.

'Father always used to buy the biggest pigs he could find – they'd weigh seven or eight stone when he brought them home. Then we'd feed them till they weighed seventeen or eighteen stone apiece and then we'd take them to market. They were so fat that one dropped dead as it walked up the ramp into the cart!

'Most of the feed we were able to buy came on the train to Drayton which was three miles away and it was a full day's work to take a cart there to collect the feed and get it back to the farm.

'I went with father once to Welshpool and he bought every single pig in the market. One lot in a pen had great long snouts and I told father I thought they'd do no good. "They're the best of the bunch" he said, and he was right.'

The pig was the great saving of many farmers and smallholders. It was a hardy animal that grew quickly and could be relied on enthusiastically to hoover up any and every kind of vegetable waste and turn it into delicious bacon.

'We loved it when we killed a pig,' remembers Reg. 'And though that will sound terrible to some people you have to remember that a lot of people went hungry then and we had no time for sentimentality. When we killed a pig we ate every last bit of it. We had liver and kidneys, sausages, pork pies were made from some bits, pork scratchings from the skin.

'After a day's work in the farmyard, mucking out or cleaning a pig carcase, we'd be covered in farm muck of one sort or another, but we only rarely had a change of trousers. Trousers were just trousers and we wore them all the time whatever their state – and there were no wellies or overalls. When you came in you just sat by the fire and the muck dried on you and steamed away. No one thought anything of it. It was just the way things were. Sometimes my trousers were so stiff with muck that they'd stand up on their own when I took them off!'

And if the standards of human hygiene were a little lower than they are now, the same is undoubtedly true of food production. In many ways the good old days of pre-industrial farming were anything but idyllic as Reg explains.

'We used to let the cows out into the fields to water before we had water piped to the sheds. Well, as they went out through the narrow gateways where all the muck and slurry would accumulate, they'd inevitably get into a terrible mess. We used to just wipe their udders with an old piece of sacking and you can imagine what the milk was like after that! When we stopped making cheese on the farm we started to sell the milk to the chocolate company Nestlé. Well, I can tell you the milk was damn near like chocolate when we sent it to them! They were always writing to father to complain so we started to wash the cows properly, but I don't think it really made a lot of difference.'

Milking was a year-round job. Haymaking on the other hand was the highlight of the summer season. Haymaking used to last from about mid-June to about the end of September. Rain was an obvious problem at haymaking time, but too much sun could make it difficult too. Reg recalls cutting a fourteen acre field.

'It was so hot that before I could get it in cocks [small piles of hay with vertical sides and a rounded top] it was what we called over made – meaning it was too dry. We started to cart it in the horse wagon, but we had a heck of a game it was so brittle. It started to fall off every time we had half a load on and I don't think there was much goodness left in it anyway.'

In more remote parts of the country, even than Shropshire, some farmers continued the traditions of the past well beyond the 1960s. Jo White who farmed all his life on the edge of Dartmoor, is a case in point. Even by the mid 1980s his farm looked pretty much as it would have done a century earlier although the horses had gone.

Joe never used chemicals or nitrates on his land – 'makes the grass grow too fast to be any good' he said – and he was unstinting in his praise of farming with horses. 'You cannot beat a horse. A horse is a wonderful

31

32    *A view looking north to the Thames Valley across the Berkshire Downs.*

*Dartmoor harvest. In the south-west the old ways lingered on into the late 1960s.* 33

34    *Suffolk Punches by the cart lodge at Cressing Temple, Essex.*

animal and don't let anyone tell you t'otherwise – even ploughing wasn't as hard as people make out with a horse. It's just quicker with a tractor, but why that's such a great thing I don't understand. It's all fast and faster today, but what this rushing is all for I don't know. Everyone wants to do everything in a hurry. Why? What are they going to do with all the time they'll have left?'

Among the ancient stone barns dotted about Joe's hundred-acre farm were the carts and ploughs, winnowing machines and mechanical potato pullers that his father and grandfather used. If you'd asked him why he kept them he would have looked at you as if you were mad because, 'no real farmer would get rid of 'em – I might use 'em again. Most of them still work and you never know – I might have to use them again!' In a granite building, that once housed a stone walkway for a horse to go round in endless circles pulling a chaff cutter mechanism, Joe still had the cart his father used every week to take the farm produce to market in nearby Chagford.

'It's just as my father left it. We call it a butt cart or a tip-up cart because when there's no horse in the shafts it tips right over! We used to take it regularly into town till quite recently. Look what a beautiful made thing it is. Each joint in the wheels and frame handmade.'

Some farmers, unlike Jo White, were, however, keen to embrace the new technology – Lance Whitehead for example remembered the first tractors coming to his Kentish farm.

'The first Fordson was built just before the Great War but it wasn't updated till 1944 and even then the updated model had only three gears. We used the D2, but even with that great tank of a thing ploughing was tough going.

'All the mowers and binders and reaping machines were powered then by the movement of their own wheels – modern equipment has power for the wheels and power for the binder or whatever it is – so if the wheels slipped on the ground you lost power. These early machines were pulled by horses, too, so there wasn't much traction and hence power anyway. They were odd looking things too, with drive belts running all over the place.'

But even in the late 1940s and 1950s much farm work in Lance's part of Kent was still done by hand or with the help of horses.

'It wasn't most of the work here – it was all the work, or that's how it seemed anyway. It was only the creation of pools of machinery by the War Office that began to change everything because more and more farmers were able to use them and get over their old prejudice against anything new-fangled.'

By today's standards, of course, early mechanical agricultural equipment seems positively antediluvian, but for farmers like Lance they represented some relief from back-breaking physical labour.

'The old binders were useful but unwieldy. They had a six-foot-wide cut and they were too big to go straight through a field gate – they had to be towed through sideways. A winding handle lowered the driving wheel once the thing was in position and when you did this the wheels on which it ran were lifted off the ground. The machine stayed still and we brought the corn to it.

'I remember when it first arrived it took us all day to work out how to set it up and use it! A big cog on the driving wheel to the main chain drove the blades and sweeps. The hay was lifted onto a canvas conveyer then lifted onto an elevator over the driving mechanism to the other side where it was packed into sheaves. Finally a knotter was activated. The whole thing was adjustable and you set the height according to the height of the crop. Unlike a modern combine harvester, the one we used seemed to involve men everywhere operating levers or rushing about adjusting things.

'Before you could use the old binders the field still had to be "opened up" by hand – a man would scythe a wide path right round the field and then the tractor had enough room to tow the machine round the field to harvest the rest of the crop.'

Like most small farmers, Lance and his brother couldn't afford to buy a machine so they hired one each year at harvest time. The brothers also kept pigs and poultry as well as cattle, and they grew corn. All the hay was turned by hand.

'We raked it into rows having cut it using our old Fordson tractor and a converted horse mower. Eventually we built it into a rick – now that was a very skilled business. We'd first put faggots – bundles of sticks – on the ground, to keep the hay up off the damp soil. Building the thing was pretty tricky – we'd work round a central pile of hay which was always kept higher than the outside edge and gradually the thing would rise from the ground. The idea was to keep the rick slightly domed to keep the rain running off quickly. And the theory is that each pitch of hay holds down the one below.'

35

36    *Seeding time in the Cotswolds.*

*Building a hay rick was a skilled, time-consuming business.* 37

38    *Under a summer sky of cumuli, stooks of oats stand near Burford on the Oxfordshire/Gloucestershire border.*

That was the theory, but as Lance laughingly confessed things didn't always go as planned and a wayward hayrick could be a terror.

'We had some disasters – sometimes the rick would seem fine until we'd almost finished it and then, almost without warning, the whole lot would begin to lean and then you were in real trouble. You could prop it up if you were lucky but the effect of the great weight was hugely exacerbated by any tendency to lean one way or another and once it had started to lean it might quickly all avalanche over into a great untidy pile. But I'm sure it happened now and then to the best of farmers.

'When we piled the hay onto the wagon it was just as bad sometimes – wagon loads of hay weren't always those neat things you see in paintings. You might have to pull the cart back to the rick yard with a couple of men holding the hay in with sticks from one side.

'Once the rick was built it would be given a proper thatched roof just like a house roof. The weight of hay on hay meant it ended up packed very tight – which is why chunks had to be cut out with a special hay knife. With re-seeded hay, hollow stems meant that after a few weeks all the hollow would be crushed out of the hay and the rick that had been ten or twelve feet high would have sunk to head height.

'In our first winter on the farm my brother and I grew three tons of absolutely useless hay – it was so bad that we had to buy in the hay for our few cattle.

'And it was hard work milking then, although we had only a few animals, because you had to milk at least twice a day and sometimes three times if you wanted the maximum yield of milk. We'd put the milk in churns and take them up to the end of the lane where they were collected by the milk lorry. It's all much easier now with tankers and sterile tanks and so on.'

The massive difference in the profitability of farming between the 1940s and 50s and the present can be judged by the market for milk, as Lance explains.

'Although we started with a couple of house cows – from which we never sold any milk – we eventually had about twelve and we could make a reasonable living from their milk. At one time we survived by selling the milk from just four cows. Real subsistence stuff!

'Most of our corn was grown for the cattle, but we also grew oats and beans. We kept the straw for the animals' bedding. We got our first milking machine in 1952 – it cost £150 and it's the only thing I've ever had on hire purchase!

'We used to get up at 6 o'clock – not really early by farming standards – and one of us would milk the cows while the other fed the calves and pigs. Then we'd go into the house for breakfast before getting out again to clean out the cowshed. If it was haymaking time we'd then perhaps spend the morning turning a piece that had been mowed – we eventually stopped doing it by hand when we bought a hay-turning machine for £5. Balers were just starting to appear then, but we used our old hay turner – it was just a couple of wheels and a series of rakes that moved to one side and flipped the hay over. You had to turn the hay like this in the field to make sure it was dry before you took it to be ricked.

'My brother tended to do the ploughing and harrowing and then we'd both do the hoeing – incredibly back-breaking work in the days before weed-killers. My back has never been the same since. All the planting we did by hand. We sowed by hand, too, using a box with two handles that had an iron wheel. As you pushed it along it popped the seeds out. It was such slow, laborious work – we just couldn't cope with it in the end. All farm work then was laborious. We used to make huge piles of mangles and then pulp them by hand mixed with chaff and oats to feed the cattle – and that had to be done every day. The cattle absolutely loved it!'

Animals were central to farming on that most remote corner of southern England at Romney Marsh. Here the marshmen flourished in a society governed by very different rules from those that applied elsewhere. Richard Body spent his life farming on the marsh. He remembers the vast, rich grazing and the early bite, as good spring grass was known, which was produced by deliberately allowing the meadows to flood in winter. This warmed the soil as well as nourishing it and the early grass was eagerly sought by farmers further inland who brought their animals down to fatten them. The marsh farmers still call these men hill farmers although their land would hardly, by most people's standards, be classed as particularly hilly. But then everything is hilly compared to the marsh.

The hill farmers hired men to look after their cattle and sheep, and shepherds in the area are still called 'lookers' by the local people. In the old days the lookers were paid so much an acre per year.

Richard was keen to emphasise just how much difference half a century has made to life on Romney Marsh.

'Take crops, for example. They were dealt with in a

39

totally different way in those days because everything was done by hand and it was laborious – all crops were sold by the bushel, a measure of volume, not weight. That meant that when you filled a bag with corn you had to be careful about the way you did it – if you did it badly the corn would sink too far into the bag and you'd have to put more in! There was a special skill in filling a bushel sack properly so that buyer and seller were happy that they'd received a fair amount. And if the corn was damp it had to be turned by hand to dry it. That, like most farm jobs, was back-breaking work. When corn was threshed it was always by four-bushel sacks. Sacks were so important in those days that merchants and farmers who didn't have their own used to hire them from firms set up solely to hire out sacks. There was, I recall, a company up in London in Tooley Street called Starkie Room who did this.

'If you sent Starkie a postcard on the Monday saying you wanted such and such number of sacks they'd be at Romney station the next day or at most a day after that. There were two goods trains a day arriving at the station at that time and every passenger train had a couple of goods wagons attached. The railway disappeared in the mid 1960s; even the tracks are gone. Crops were once sold in what probably seem odd amounts now – corn for example was always sold by the quarter – that is two sacks containing eight bushels.'

Richard always loved the machinery of farming whether mechanical or horse-drawn and he was something of an expert on the carts of Sussex and elsewhere.

'On our farm we had big old high-sided carts for moving things around and the normal calculation was one horse per ton load. Each district made its own style of wagon and there were different types for different conditions – narrow-wheeled carts were used in dry weather and broad-wheeled when it was wet to prevent the cart getting bogged down in the mud.

'I remember on one occasion, I think it would have been in the 1940s, when we were carrying corn over very wet ground. We had a broad-wheeled wagon but even with a one-horse load – about one ton of stuff – we could only just budge it using two horses. Even then it was almost axle deep in the mire and the horses were straining to move it.

'There was a wagon maker at Ashford but we always bought ours second-hand as did most of the farmers – I remember I paid £4 for one once. Our wagons had poles sticking up vertically along the sides – we called wagons like this standards. The poles held the hay or corn or whatever in and you could then pile it up much higher than the sides of the wagon without the risk of it toppling out all over the place.'

On Romney Marsh the coming of winter meant the usual ditch clearing work but there was also reed-cutting to be done. Richard again:

'The reeds grew in and along the ditches, but marsh reed is not like Norfolk reed which is cut when the flag is off. We cut it in winter and then stored it carefully to thatch corn- and hay-stacks, and even cottages.'

With so much flat, even ground Romney Marsh attracted some of the earliest modern farm equipment. Huge, laborious steam-driven threshers and balers might seem antique by today's standards but they were revolutionary when they first appeared.

'In this area we had the right sort of ground to use the early steam ploughs and threshers. There were half a dozen or more sets of steam tackle that toured the marsh and beyond – individual farmers hired the tackle for as long as they needed it and we were charged £1 per acre. By 1922 my father – always keen on new things and being in control of his own farm and its equipment – had bought his own steam plough tackle, but we still had horses for ploughing – partly because at one stage though we had a steam plough we couldn't find a driver for it!

'With a steam plough you set up the two parts of the thing at either side of the field and then the plough itself is drawn back and forth between the two pieces of machinery using pulleys and conveyors. The steam plough machine itself didn't move.'

Steam ploughs were cumbersome and expensive, however, so horses were still used wherever and whenever they could make a better job of it.

'We used the horses to plough in winter what we couldn't plough in summer. We had two four-horse teams – this was four-horse team ground – in other words the land was too heavy for a two-horse team. Horses could plough about an acre a day and it was a very skilled business, if you were to get it right and with the furrows all in line and allowance left for drainage. There was a wagoner and a mate for each team and they had to cut their own chaff for their horses every evening.

'Steam ploughs could do ten acres a day compared to one for a horse team, so you can see the advantage they had, but our ground was pretty stiffish and horses did more elsewhere. We used two main types of plough with the horses. The balance plough which was iron and the

*Young cattle in their warm yard at Ashwells Farm, Terling, Essex. The farmer is John Tarlton's brother, David.* 41

*Arthur Rush of Great Leighs, Essex, was eighty years old when this photograph was taken in the 1950s. His father and grandfather were shepherds and it is likely that his line goes back to the days when England's wealth depended on the wool trade. He sits on the steps of his shepherd's hut feeding an orphan lamb.*

*Devon reds, a breed of cattle that has now almost disappeared, grazing by the River Tamar, Cornwall.* 43

*Steam ploughing in Essex. The five-furrow plough is being hauled by a Fowler engine.*

jack plough which was all-wood except for the tip of the plough share and had no wheels. We used the jack plough when the ground was very wet because, being lighter, it didn't get bogged down as easily as the iron balance plough. Every part of the country had its own distinctive design of plough – on the hills just off the marsh we used a plough with two wheels, for example, that was very different from anything used on the marsh. But the balance and jack ploughs we used are almost identical to ploughs I have seen illustrated in books about medieval farming!'

One of the hardest jobs on the farm was the simple task of getting water to where it was needed. On Richard's farm it had to be carried everywhere in buckets – for the pigs, the cattle, the thresher. The farm workers took buckets down to the pond and simply dipped them in, but the bulk of the work was done by Richard and his brothers.

'The work was so hard that every term I put on weight while at school at Hastings and then lost it when I came back to the farm in the holidays.

'People – farmworkers in particular – liked to work on the marsh because we traditionally paid sixpence or a shilling a week more than they paid in other areas. But there were disadvantages – what people used to call the ague was always bad here because of the damp and the water. Until well into this century you could buy laudanum in the local shops to treat it. Laudanum is an opium derivative and it was the only thing that would alleviate the terrible effects of the mosquitoes before the coming of chemicals to control them.

'We did have another experiment to control the mosquitoes – a chap introduced some kind of Hungarian frog which multiplied and thrived – you still find them everywhere – but they reduced the numbers of mosquitoes dramatically.

*Friesian heifers in the yard at Crab Farm, Shapwick, Dorset.* 45

*Moving to fresh pastures, at Shapwick, Dorset. The flock of four hundred ewes on an early June morning lead by Michael Tory, whose great-great-grandfather founded the Hampshire Down breed, in the same parish, in 1834.*

On Richard's farm ten men were once employed full-time, but by the mid 1980s not a single man was employed.

'Until the horses went we had a chap who worked with a wagon for carting and fetching worsels, we had a chap who looked after the sheep, another chap who drove the vanner – a horse that could trot a bit and pull three-quarters of a ton on the level. That was a lighter wagon that we generally used for farm work. We also had a thatcher here full time and a stacker – for the haystacks.

'If it was a real wet day the wagoner or his mate took horses that needed shoeing to the forge where, of course, others would have gathered for the same reason so there would be a queue and a long wait. I can remember the men standing in under the covered part of the building well out of the rain, but with their shoulders protected by sacking. They always enjoyed it because they could have a good old chat while they waited.'

It is easy to forget that, just like the modern car, the old farm cart was by no means maintenance free, as Richard explains.

'Another important job for the wagoner was to grease all the wagon- and cart-wheels. This was normally a two-man job. The carts were great heavy things and each wheel had to be jacked up in turn. The lynch-pin was then taken out with what we called a lynch-pin drawer (a T-shaped tool with a claw that slid along the round, half-inch shaft). This claw hooked under the head of the pin and in the nave or hub of the wheel there was always a two-inch square gap on the outer edge to allow the pin to be pulled right out. The wheel was then slid off the axle and a good layer of thick cart grease – made from horse and other animal bones – was smeared onto the top part of the axle. The wheel would then be lifted back onto the axle in such a way as to leave as much grease as possible on top of the axle. Then the inside edge of the pin had to be greased and driven back into its hole in the axle. Before the jack was lowered the wheel was carefully spun to distribute the grease evenly. I remember the grease was always either thick black or a dirty yellow colour. Before the job was finished it was very important that the lock was greased. The lock was the part on which the shafts turned and if it wasn't well greased the horses would find it difficult to turn the cart.

'If he was travelling hilly country the wagoner knew that it was his responsibility to remember to take a skidpan with him. This was used to stop the wagon running away with a heavy load as it went downhill. For hilly country the wagoner would also need to be properly equipped for holding his wagon if the horses needed a blow – a breather – when going up the hill. Sometimes a wooden block would be used for this, but better still a wooden roller about six inches in diameter. This would be hung behind the rear near wheel. Wagons were never fitted with brakes. At the bottom of a hill you had to be very careful about taking off the skidpan because it would be searingly hot from the friction of the road and many a man received a bad burn by forgetting this.'

Back on the farm, winter brought some slightly more unusual tasks including, of all things, sack mending.

'Wherever the sacks were hung in a barn the rats and mice were always able to find them and nest in them. Sacks were made to carry four bushels; some were made of soft jute, others of a cotton and jute mix. These were the best sacks. Soft balls of string called fillis were used to mend the sacks, but binder twine was an alternative and there was a real skill to the business. You used a needle with a curved, flattened and extremely sharp tip. This was used to make a ring of loops round the edge of a hole; then another slightly smaller series of loops was joined to that first ring and so on until the hole filled. You couldn't do it the way you'd darn socks or it would have no strength at all.'

Richard also remembers the hay buyers who toured the farms to buy fodder for the hay markets and who were enormously skilled when it came to testing their wares.

'All hay buyers carried an iron rod with them about six feet long with a barb near the tip. The rod was pushed into the stack and when pulled out again the barb would hang on to a small sample from the centre of the stack. The idea was that the buyer could then see and smell what the stack was really like in the middle. The rod was also used to test if the stack was too hot. If it had been stacked too green or too damp the hay could get so hot that it would very likely burst into flames. If the rod came out and the end was too hot to touch – which did happen – then the buyer knew that the stack had reached the danger point and had to be turned or cut out.'

Life on a marsh farm was hard, but in that respect at least, it was very much the same right across the marsh, particularly in the days when the roads were still unmade.

'Pebbles and stones from the beach were used to surface all the marsh roads until long after the Great War ended and indeed on the smaller lanes they continued to be used until well after the Second World War.

'Rock was brought down into the marsh from Lympne or Aldington for other, bigger roads and then broken up into small pieces by old men wearing wire-gauze glasses. This broken rock would be spread over the road to be re-surfaced and then well steamrollered to make it level. A certain length of the beach lanes was macadamed like this each year and in summer in the heat these roads grew white and dusty; in winter they turned into a sea of white mud.'

It is difficult today to comprehend quite how poor the mass of people in the countryside were in the first part of the last century. But on the marsh poverty was real and ever present. Sticks were gathered by the women for firewood in the harshest weather and after the corn had been harvested the gleaners would come into the fields by ancient custom – these were women and children who gathered up odd scraps of corn to feed themselves and their families. They would go into the pastures, too, to collect scraps of wool that the sheep had shed. According to Richard this practice lasted well into the 1940s and the richest pickings were to be had round the sheep pound.

*Farmworkers by the Dutch barn: Terling, Essex.*

*Essex farmland in spring near Chelmsford.* 49

50  *A Yorkshire shepherd returns from tending his flock near Bolton Abbey in Wharfedale, Yorkshire.*

In the North-East of England the windswept uplands demanded a different sort of farming. William Wade spent his working life farming near Stockton and his fondest memories of the past – as with so many old farmers – are of the horses.

'On this farm we had between twelve and fourteen horses at any one time. We used to breed from them and when the youngsters were old enough they were sold either to work in the towns or to work down the mines. It may seem cruel today, but they were essential because there was no mechanical means to get the coal back from the face to the shafts and we needed coal – everyone did, for fires, heating and industry. Apart from wood, if you were in the country, there was nothing else.'

Before the Second World War and for some time afterwards goods were still delivered locally, too, in a region that has always seemed remote from the centres of power.

'Yes, for many years after we first came here we used to deliver all our produce locally. I remember we used to cart our wheat to a mill at Stockton about eight miles away. We sold twenty tons once and delivered it in what was called a Rolley, a great heavy four-wheeled wagon that took two tons at a time and needed two horses to pull. For this work the horses were harnessed one in front of the other, not abreast.

'Ordinary carts normally carried about a ton and we put the corn or barley in sacks. These sacks were filled differently for different crops. A sack of wheat always weighed sixteen stone, barley eighteen stone, beans twenty-two stone and so on.'

The last few Long Newton horses hung on for general carting until about 1960.

William loved working with them because they'd always go without being driven and they knew exactly what they were doing and what was wanted of them. They only had to do a task a few times to pick it up.

'They used to walk between the stooks of corn and they'd stop in just the right place without being told so that we could lift the hay onto the wagon.'

William was fascinated by the range of carts available and the regional variations in their design.

'Scottish carts were very different from English. The Scottish cart had a lot of iron in it where the English cart was almost entirely of wood. Irish carts had shafts back and front. The Irish also had special long, high-sided carts for the hay and I remember going to Ireland with my father to buy cattle before the war and seeing fifteen or maybe twenty long Irish hay carts slowly moving along the road towards Dublin. High up on the hay on every single wagon sat groups of men drinking and playing nap. That was a glorious sight.

'Up here in the North-East the roads were all unmade until after the Second World War and even then a lot of the minor ones were left as tracks. No one really had responsibility for the upkeep of the roads – it was just as it had been centuries before so we used to try to keep the roads near us as well surfaced as we could by going to collect cinders from a factory on Teeside. We'd cart the cinders and then spread them over the potholes and ruts. It gave the cartwheels something to bite into.'

As they bred their own horses for work on the farm William's family had a strict routine for training them.

'We always started to train a young horse sometime around Christmas. I don't know why but that was the time. You got the horse used to being handled and then put a bit on it. When it was used to that you harnessed it in the middle of three horses harnessed abreast. That way it was penned in by two old, quiet experienced horses that would keep it right. At first you kept a young horse in harness for only half a day at a time because they would get sore shoulders if you didn't do it slowly and gradually. You also had to make sure you had a good, well-fitting collar for the horse. There was a real skill to making a good collar that wouldn't rub. We went to the local saddler for that – he made just about everything and anything to do with leather and he would make a one-off for a horse with an odd-shaped neck.

'For ploughing we had only two instructions for the horses – we'd shout "haa" if we wanted the horse to turn right and "gee back" if we wanted it to turn left. Horses were harnessed abreast for ploughing in many areas, but here I often ploughed with a team of three in line. The quickest was always at the front and the strongest at the back or in the heel position, because turning at the headlands relied on the back horse and it was hard work for her.

'A horse-drawn plough is difficult to control at first because it must cut in a straight line and to an even depth – not easy when you think that while you concentrate on these things you also have to concentrate on three great horses. We used a wheeled plough which was easier, but my father – a champion ploughman in his time – used a most difficult plough which had no wheels at all.'

51

*After the harvest; stooks in a field in Norfolk before the War.*

William recalled that trade with Ireland from the North-East was brisk and also that on several occasions he took delivery of Irish cattle – 'they were always fine beasts,' he says – and then drove them along the roads to Long Newton.

'I remember bringing about thirty cattle from the railway station twenty miles away. We'd bought them in Ireland and I had the dog to help me, but twenty miles along rough roads is a long way to drive that many cattle in a day. By the time we'd got half way back to the farm the dog's pads were worn away and its feet were bleeding so I had to put it over my shoulders and carry it.'

Rowley Blundell who began farming in north Wales just after the Great War also had vivid memories of driving animals along the roads.

'Like all farmers we walked all our animals to market. To get from our farm to Denbigh with twenty or thirty sheep would take about two and a half hours, but many times we'd drive the sheep there, fail to sell them and have to drive them all the way back again! And with geese on the old drovers' roads, we would dab their feet in pitch before we set off so they wouldn't wear out and bleed on the stony track.'

Back on the east coast of England, John Elgey remembered the hiring fairs in the Wolds region of Yorkshire where his family had farmed for generations. The fairs were a sort of primitive labour exchange where farm workers were contracted to work for a year.

'We normally had twelve men living and working here at any one time. Most of these men were got from

*Arthur Chanter has worked for more than twenty-five years as a saddler and harness maker in Dulverton, Somerset. He is making a bull's show headcollar.*     53

54 *Dartington Hall Farms, Devon. The Barton Herd of ninety British Friesians going into afternoon's milking. Dartington Hall can be glimpsed in the distance.*

the hiring fair – fairs were held all over the country in the market towns, usually in November, and men who wanted to be hired would walk around slowly, perhaps with a bit of straw sticking out of a pocket or in a lapel. It's only now that the days of the hiring fair are gone that I realise what an ancient and in many ways strange way they were to hire your workforce.'

The system with horses in John's part of the world was rather different from that which held sway elsewhere, but John's farm was bigger than average and needed a hierarchy of horsemen.

'The head horseman or wagoner had his own stable, by which I mean he was completely in control of it – with six horses and what was called a wagoner's lad, his assistant really. Under the wagoner's lad was the third lad (there was no second lad for some reason!) then came the fourth lad and sometimes what we called the little lad or box lad.

'It was quite a team, but the horses had to be looked after properly because they ran the farm. The wagoner supervised all those under him, and above the wagoner was the farm foreman. The workers might include two or three married men from the village who walked up to us every day or we'd hire single men at the hiring fair. The hiring fair in November – Martinmas week – was at Driffield. And there we'd hire men for a year with the stipulation that they could have one week off. Not very generous I know by today's standards, but it was the way all farmers did it then.

'The workmen would always ask "Is it a good meat house?" – meaning would they get plenty to eat. Some would want to know how much salmon they would have to eat – that was a serious question because farms on estates where there were salmon rivers were often fed on fish from the river every day for weeks through the summer and they didn't like it. Or up towards Whitby they'd worry that the farmer would give

*The farmer tests the tilth for barley. Spring, Essex.*

them sea fish every day because it was cheaper than meat.'

John explained that men at the hiring fair were almost always taken on for the year and that meant that if they left after six months they weren't paid a penny. They received their full wages at the end of the year, and nothing at all in the meantime, but it was a system that had been handed down for generations and it was unquestioned.

55

56    *Exmoor sheep sale. Pens of sheep being filled up before the auction starts.*

*Expert hedger Willy Spratt at work near Roasby, Leicestershire.*　57

'Some men were happy where they worked – our foreman and his wife, for example, stayed with us for thirty-seven years. The foreman's wife used to cook for the men – all twelve used to sleep in one big bedroom which we called the dormitory. Two men slept to a bed and the foreman's maid made the beds every day. It all seems like another world now, but that's the way it was.

'For most of the winter we would be ploughing because it was a slow old business then, but it gave a lot of men employment through the long winter months. There wasn't much else to do in the cold months except perhaps keeping an eye on the sheep, bringing the turnips in for them, hedging and ditching, and a hundred and one other things! Roving bands of Irishmen would come each year to offer to do the hedging and ditching. They slept rough mostly and Lord knows how they made a living going from farm to farm doing it. It was very hard work digging out the mud and slime and laying or cutting the hedge.

'A good team of men might lay a hundred feet of hedge in a day. It was a really skilled business because the upright shoots in the hedge had to be carefully selected and then cut three-quarters of the way through – any more and they would almost certainly die. You wanted them cut through just enough to make sure you could bend them down till they were parallel with the ground. Stakes were driven into the ground at intervals of a few feet and then the pleachers – the three-quarters-severed uprights – would be brought down and woven through the stakes. The result looked a bit bleak in winter – a bit like a sort of woven basket about three feet high – but when the branches started to shoot the following spring you had a marvellous stock-proof hedge that was always thick at the base. Modern hedges, where they haven't been taken out, are often gappy and thin near the ground because of the modern hedge cutters which just smash the tops off.'

After winter ploughing and spring sowing came harvest time, the high point of the farming year. Until the 1950s massive ricks were built and John still has a photograph showing the last rick at his farm – a testament, as he says, to a skill already by then in its death throes.

'Some of the threshing was done straight after harvest and the rest spread through the winter. We used a steam thresher that had been introduced in the nineteenth century. You just fed the sheaves of barley or whatever from the rick into it – the men who did this work were known as stackers. Most of the winter threshing was done after the wheat was sown in December. We'd do about forty days threshing then – one or two days a week or whatever. It generally had all been done by April, except perhaps the last stack of oats which was kept for the horses.

'Until about 1950 everything was brought into the stackyard where – obviously enough – it was stacked by the stackman. He laid the sheaves when they came in off the wagon and the technique was rather like bricklaying. It was as if he was building a wall. The middle was always kept slightly fuller than the outside and what we called a spread fork was used for the work. It was slightly different in design from a pitchfork, less likely to hold the hay and better for spreading.

'The hayrick itself, well – it was a bit like a long, low house. It had to be perfectly symmetrical and the outside sheaves had to be at the correct angle if the whole thing was to be watertight, and if it wasn't watertight it was worse than useless. Some stacks had perpendicular ends, others round ends. If we were building a big stack it would take all day, but the rick builders were kept busy because we used three wagons right through the day. One was always being loaded in the field, one was always on the road to the stackyard and one was always being unloaded. One man stayed on the stack to build it and one man, sometimes two, forked up the sheaves to the builder. At the eaves the stack might be ten feet tall.

'Come the spring we would start drilling and cultivating, probably in early March if it was dry enough. Then it was all hands to the harrowing. We might finish by April and there might be a little late ploughing into April for the turnips.

'After April if you grew spuds you would plant them and then, in early June, we'd sow a few more turnips. As the crops started to come up we were kept busy chopping out the weeds – weeds were bad then without chemicals to control them. It was a full-time job just to keep on top of them.

'The farming year was very repetitive, but what we did was based on the experience of generations and little variation was ever even thought about, though we might vary one or two tasks by a month or so according to the state of the weather.'

While the arable year moved gradually on, the sheep and other animals still had to be looked after. The sheep were sheared at the end of May or the beginning of June and though the Elgeys employed a full-time shepherd on

*Exmoor farmer John Woollacott with his Exmoor Horn sheep.* 59

*A winter store of potatoes. Although these King Edwards were harvested during wet weather they were protected from frost by lining the walls with straw bales.*

the farm, there was so much extra work that they had to employ extra labour to help the shepherd. And of course, as with everything else the farmer's sons had to help too.

'But if times were hard for us they were very hard indeed for the farmworkers. They had a terrible time and though I think and hope we treated them as well as we could, they were often so poor that many couldn't even afford a bicycle; the cowman walked a mile from the village every day and though he started at seven he was never late and he worked through till six. When the clocks changed he ignored them because messing about with time had no effect on the cows and therefore none on his work. Robert Harper was his name.'

The number of farmworkers who died, worn out and broken by the lack of work and by endless grinding poverty in the period between the wars is difficult to calculate. But with only the most rudimentary system of welfare there is no doubt that tens of thousands of families in remote rural areas scraped by at a level of poverty quite unimaginable today. They might only have had soup made with potato peelings for days on end; for fuel they would have to scour the woods and fields for sticks, and the head of the family might disappear for weeks on end tramping miles and sleeping in haystacks in search of a few days' work. Poverty can never have been easy to bear, but there is little doubt that people's expectations of a reasonable standard of living were lower in the early part of the last century.

*An Essex meadow under the summer sky.*

62    *Beer and dominoes. A quiet game in an old Essex pub.*

# 3.
# COUNTRY CHARACTERS

Before television, motorways and easier communications eroded the strong sense of regional identity that once existed in various parts of Britain, country people were an extraordinarily mixed bunch – far more so than they are today when villages empty each morning as their inhabitants set off for their office jobs in the nearest town. When country people lived and worked locally they were far more likely to develop into real characters; into people with a strong sense of their own identity. Those who lived in out-of-the-way villages and hamlets or on remote farms did things as they chose and worried little about how they were perceived in the wider world. They were part of the local scene and however eccentric their behaviour might sometimes become, they were accepted.

Kent farmer Aubrey Charman remembered one noted character whose eccentricity amounted to little more than being extremely antisocial.

'Bernard Green died in 1979. He would have been about seventy-five, I think, but I remembered him from when he was about twenty and he came to work for my father. He was a most conscientious worker but nothing would induce him to get to work before nine o'clock and as that upset all the other farm workers who started at seven o'clock we had to get rid of him.

'When he left he rented about twenty acres of land and reared stock. He would help any farmer at harvest time. He was often seen digging potatoes late at night by the light of a lamp, but you'd never see him doing it during daylight. He never mixed with the villagers and lived in some poverty in a cottage down an overgrown lane. He was often seen returning from his cattle well after midnight.

'When he was found dead he was in bed with his overcoat and boots on, and scattered all around him were cattle sales cheques going back years. He'd never bothered to pay them into the bank. Although he lived in Southwater for more than sixty years I don't suppose he was known to more than twenty people and he had no friends.'

Most country people escaped the routine of farm work every now and then in the village pub. With little in the way of entertainment the local pub was usually the sole source of regular pleasure and amusement. Inevitably it attracted – and produced – some very rum characters.

Shropshire farmer Reg Dobson recalled the antics of his maternal grandfather, a trained blacksmith who shod all the horses on local farms. He also had a great fondness for beer and every Wednesday he'd set off for the nearest market town – in this case Market Drayton.

'He'd always take the horse and wagon – or float as we used to call it. He'd invariably take his neighbour, who was an old friend, with him. The two would disappear slowly down the dusty, leafy road. They'd put the horse up at the pub – every pub had stables then – and then proceed to get gloriously drunk. At chucking-out time the old publican would help the two of them out the door and into the wagon. He'd lead the horse into the middle of the street and away they would go. After no more than a hundred yards grandfather and his friend would fall fast asleep in the bottom of the wagon and the old horse would slowly make his way home five miles away. The horse would walk into the yard where he would stop until my grandma came out to wake the two men and give them a good telling off. The telling off never did any good. The following week they'd be off again.'

Then there was Uncle Arthur.

'He was another old bugger – one of the first in our area to get a car, but it was such an old banger that we used to have to get a horse to pull it before it would start. I once went with him in the car and he drove twenty miles on the wrong side of the road. If he met a wagon or another car (very rare) he would simply curse and yell at the other driver as if it was his fault that we were on the wrong side of the road.'

Reg's father was an early motoring enthusiast. In the 1920s he bought a one-cylinder Rover. When he went to collect it the garage owner showed him how to steer it and how to start it but forgot to explain the small matter of getting the thing to stop.

'Dad just got in it and drove off in fits and starts thinking he was doing very well for a first timer. All went well until he reached Myrtle Bank which was a very steep hill. About half-way down he realised he was going like hell and didn't know how to stop it. In his panic he obviously reacted as he would in a wagon – he pulled on the wheel like mad and shouted 'Whoa!' at the top of his voice. Of course, it did no good and he shot into the ditch at the bottom of the hill. He was lucky not to be injured.'

Reg Boffey was another Shropshire character who was locally famous throughout the 1940s. He did odd jobs and lived on almost nothing in a remote tumble-down cottage.

When a cow was dying one night in a barn the farmer asked Reg to sit up all night and give her regular doses of whisky on the off-chance that she might rally round. When the farmer got up the next morning the cow was very dead and Reg was fast asleep and as drunk as a lord. He later said he thought it was a waste of good Scotch to give it to the cow!

Then there was Rollie. He used to tour the farms at haymaking time and sleep every night in the stable, as north Wales farmer Rowley Williams recalls.

'When he came to milk he'd run from one cow to the next and always have finished all his animals before anyone else had finished theirs. If he took a pair of horses out chain harrowing he'd damn near kill them

he'd drive them so hard. One of our neighbours once offered Rollie five shillings an acre to spread five acres of muck. Rollie had finished by early afternoon so he went into the local village and drank all his money – twenty-five shillings was a hell of a lot in those days when beer was fourpence a pint. I don't know how he drank that much without killing himself. This all happened on a Saturday and he didn't come to milk on the Sunday. We discovered later that he'd slept it off in a ditch – he never seemed to mind where he slept.'

For Reg Dobson one of the great pleasures of country life was the range of characters and the things they got up to – at one end of the spectrum was the eccentric, at the other, the mad, bad and positively illegal. But they were always – or nearly always – fun.

'Banker Tew was one of the great workers round about, particularly at harvest time. He'd lost one hand in a chaff cutter as a young man, but he could wield a fork with the best of them.

'Banker was always arguing with Mrs Clark, the landlady of the local pub. One Sunday it got so bad that they stood and almost screamed at each other. Mrs Clark was foaming at the mouth. Banker was a lot taller – she was only about four feet – so I put her on a chair. She was so worked up that she didn't even notice when I lifted her and she just carried on (but face to face now) arguing with Banker.'

People often loved their work so much, despite low pay and dire conditions, that they would do far more than was really necessary.

'Another great character I haven't mentioned was Tom Bennett, the champion hedge-layer of the whole of Shropshire. If he didn't get first prize for the best hedge-laying one year he'd get it for the best grown hedge the next. Every job he did was perfect and he didn't care how long he spent on a job to get it right. He used to cut our lawn with a scythe as good as any modern lawnmower could do it. He was a great rick builder, too, and when he'd finished he'd often come back at night to pull out the loose bits of hay just to make sure it looked perfect. I can still see him lamp in hand looking at his work like a great artist – which of course he was.

'Tom used to chew tobacco twist and he was a deadly accurate spitter – he once hit a cat on the head at about twenty feet. And he had amazing teeth. He used to bite into an iron railing at the bottom of the garden and swing from it for relaxation.

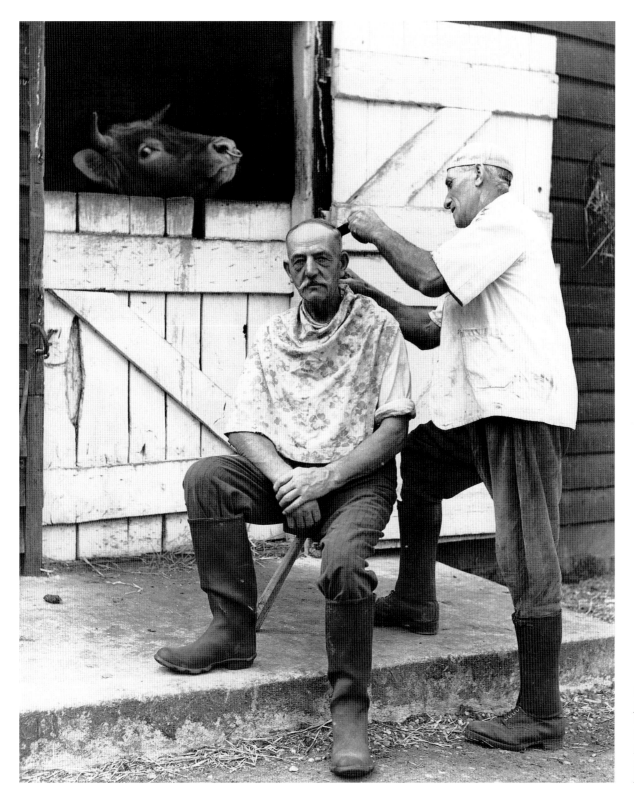

*Country
people could
turn a hand
to anything,
including an
occasional
hair cut.*

*Thatching the George Inn at Barford St Michael, North Oxfordshire. The thatcher is working on the ridge which is*
*forty feet from the ground.*

'Tom never went anywhere in his whole life to the best of my knowledge, except one trip after he retired. He got the bus to the Royal Show at Lincoln got lost, missed the bus back and spent £20 – a small fortune – on a taxi to get back. That was the first and last time he went anywhere.

'Another old character was Charlie Denton. He was a devil for telling tall tales. And if someone was arguing about something Charlie always had to have something bigger or better than everybody else.

'I went down to the local pub one night and Charlie was sitting at a table with a couple from the town. He was explaining about shooting to them. He said he had an old muzzle gun that you poured the powder into and then rammed it down with a rod. He said he forgot to take the rod out one day, fired and the rod went straight through a duck which then landed on and killed a hare.

He said he'd got such a fright at this that he'd jumped off the road into a river and come up with a couple of eels in each pocket. Then he said he had a gun that fired shot that went round a field till it hit something. By this time the locals were holding their sides, but the two townies seemed to be taking it all in, or maybe they were just being polite!

'Perhaps the funniest farm worker – but he was also incredibly hard-working – was an Irishman who worked for a neighbouring farmer. Pat was sent thistle-cutting and when the farmer went across the field a couple of hours later Pat was walking about completely naked from the waist down. "What's the idea Pat?" said the farmer, "you'll get locked up."

"I had a lot of beer last night," said Pat, "and I've got a touch of the runs and can't get my trousers down quick enough!" came the reply.'

*A trio of magnificent greys drilling Essex oats.*

68    *A traditional gipsy with her clothes-pegs sitting on the front of the caravan.*

Up in the North-East William Wade had happy memories of similar long-vanished workers.

'A chap called Walter used to work for us and he was a wonderful workman. He liked piece work and he and his wife used to dig our potatoes. They'd dig eleven square roods a day which is some going, and while they were doing it they used to camp in the field. Walter also used to pull our swedes and he was so fast there'd be one landing on the heap, one flying through the air and one in his hand. He'd go on like that all day and when we were all hoeing together he'd leave us standing if he felt like it.

'In winter he used to cut our hedges. He used a short-handled slasher and as he was six feet tall and our hedges were rather small he could cut both sides at the same time simply by leaning over. As he cut, so his wife gathered the brashings and piled them up and burned them. They were a great team, but all they got for the work was threepence a rood. By working all the hours God sends – milking, hoeing, drilling, sowing and ploughing – they made about £16 a week.'

The ancient and unique system by which Romney Marsh governed its own affairs was as eccentric as any of the characters who worked there, as Richard Body recalled.

'I am lord of the manor of Ruckinge. It doesn't mean a great deal – in fact it's so ancient and so complex that the rights and duties that attach to it are hardly understood by anyone! Dad bought it in 1921 for £50 and I inherited it when he died. I don't think he bought it to increase his standing in the area or anything like that because the lordship originally conferred more obligations than privileges – along with the bailiffs and jurats of the level of Romney Marsh we, the lords, were traditionally responsible for administering the drainage of the area and looking after the sea wall. We've lost all our responsibilities now, but we still meet each year on the Thursday of Whitsun week, at the Hall in Dymchurch and there is just enough money still coming in from let property to pay for our lunch!'

*Drilling oats at Church Farm, Naunton, Gloucestershire.*

69

Romney Marsh is the only part of England that elects its own magistrates – four annually from the jurats, who are themselves elected from the local people. There are twenty-three lordships in this part of Kent, eight or nine of which are actually in the marsh. The Lordships go back more than 1000 years.

'There were some marvellous odd characters in and around the marsh in those days. I remember Miss Banks, the retired schoolteacher. One of her treasured possessions was a horse's skull – it had pride of place in her house – and though she was a portly woman she used to pedal into New Romney to do her shopping on a tricycle pulled by a big collie dog.

'Then there was Miss Richardson who kept her bedroom absolutely full of canaries. There were hundreds of them. She never liked my father, who only had one eye – she once threatened to poke it out with a hat pin!

'There seemed to be more characters in the countryside in those days. I remember Tom Else who was quite old when I knew him fifty years ago. He was our odd-job man. He'd been kicked badly by a horse when young and was, as a result, very lame. He started working for us at Michaelmas 1912 – the hiring of men, the leasing of land and so on all began on Michaelmas day then. He used to pump the water for us from a well every day; he'd drive the trap too. He and I must have put many tons of hay on the London wagon over the years.

'Trib Boulden was a steam plough foreman and odd job man with a real talent for engineering – he used to fix the first cars that arrived down here, but he was also a real craftsman – I remember he made me a lovely chisel from a half-inch thick piece of raw metal. He also helped to repair the carriages. Trib was born and lived his whole life in the same village. He told me that as a boy he was once put in a barrel on the top of a knoll where there had been a warning beacon and then rolled down. He said he was black and blue at the end of it. He always had a bottle of cold tea with him and even in his sixties when I knew him he could lift two half hundredweights over his head – one in each hand.

'Albert Dennis was a quiet man who served right through the Great War. He was a master stack-builder and what I particularly remember about him was how hard the skin of his hands was – he could handle any sheaves of corn without gloves, no matter how full of sharp thistles they were. He was a real expert worker, but no horseman. He could do just about anything else – dipping in long-pod beans, planting turnips and so on, and he was always the man we got to mow by hand around the field before we could bring in the binder for a clear first round. He always wore leather straps around his trousers just below the knees. His trousers looked baggy as a result but they wore out more slowly – or so he claimed.'

Up on the Yorkshire Wolds John Elgey also had fond memories of a long-vanished breed of countryman.

'A carrier – a sort of travelling salesman – came to us once a week with all sorts of provisions. He'd call to collect our surplus butter and eggs and then deliver them in Driffield for us at various destinations – shops and so on. He'd tell them where the produce had come from and later on the shopkeepers would pay us. It was all done on trust. He'd shout and sing and was never embarrassed whether he had an audience or not! And he'd take anything anywhere for you. We'd pay him a certain amount for doing the carrying and that was how he made his living. Often you'd see him moving slowly along the lanes in his cart and a typical load would be two women at the front, a dead sheep in the back and a great tub of our butter balanced in the middle.

'He would take any sheep that had died on the farm – it didn't matter if it had died from illness or accident or whatever. He'd take it to a small factory in Driffield where a man would skin it and take the wool off – there was a bit of money in that – then the carcase would be put into a boiler for a few hours and the fat produced would be used for greasing wheels and axles on carts and wagons, or for making soap and face cream. I often thought of those girls carefully putting on face cream that had been made from a sheep we'd found dead in a ditch!'

# 4.

# HOUSE AND GARDEN

Things have always changed in the countryside as elsewhere, but with modern communications the pace of change in rural areas during the second half of the twentieth century accelerated beyond anything experienced in previous generations.

In 1380 a Londoner who visited the northern part of Kent found he could not understand a word the local people said – at that time you had only to travel fifty miles to realise that strong accents and changes in vocabulary and grammar made English a set of many languages. By the early twentieth century these differences had lessened but even as late as the 1970s elderly people on remote farms in Devon, for example, still spoke in a way that outsiders found impenetrable.

And if people changed little until the coming of the car and the television, the houses and farms they lived in remained surprisingly – and delightfully – old fashioned too.

Aubrey Charman, who was born around 1900, was still living in a medieval farmhouse in the 1970s and 1980s. The house, filled with furniture that had been in place since the 1830s, was known as New House but the date above the door told another story, as Aubrey explained.

'The date is 1575 and it's repeated on a carved beam inside the house. Of course there have been changes but the house is substantially now as it has always been. What used to be an external door in one wall of the 1462 part of the house is beautifully preserved after being enclosed in 1575 by the building of the new.

'This house has fifteen bedrooms and the roof space would fit two or three semi-detached houses! It's enormous and though each stone slate weighs more than a hundredweight there are so many massive oak timbers the whole thing has hardly moved in four hundred years.'

The kitchen still has its flagged stone floor and massive lead pump. The pump itself, beautifully decorated with a floral motif raised in the lead, was made when the house was built and it still works. Aubrey reveals two oak settles built into the walls of the massive fireplace above which a remarkable ancient jack spit remains. Built with a weight on a pulley the jack spit has a crude, clock-like series of wheels and gears, and with the weight attached, it will slowly turn the massive roasting spit above the fire. So ingenious is the design that the weight takes about fifteen minutes to reach the ground and all that time the housewife is able to get on with other tasks safe in the knowledge that her roasting pig will be evenly cooked on all sides!

The sixteenth century sitting room, immediately above the cellar, still has every last inch of its original oak panelling.

But Aubrey was not sentimental about every aspect of the past.

'The difficulties of the past may sound interesting today, but when modern alternatives came along I can see why people grabbed them gratefully with both hands. Take matches – well, they weren't invented till the 1850s. Before that you had to strike a flint to light anything and getting a flame from a flint wasn't easy. We

72    *A late medieval farmhouse sheltered by its stacks and trees, near Terling, Essex.*

got round the problem here by never letting the fire go out. Year after year it stayed alight, but there was a skill in making sure it stayed alight. Every night when you went to bed you covered the glowing ashes with grey burned-through ash. In the morning when you raked this grey stuff off, the red embers would still be alight and you could get the thing going again.

'We had two maids in those days who slept at the top of the house. They got up at six every morning – the same time as everyone else – and lit the big sixty-gallon copper we had for boiling water. And this copper had to be filled using buckets filled at the pump. That carried on until about 1940 when the piped water arrived.'

The weekly routine at Aubrey's farmhouse was probably typical of farms across the South-East. On Mondays the housemaid would light the big sixty-gallon copper fire with faggots – these were bundles of hazel sticks about six feet long and a foot wide – to heat the water for washing day. About 9 o'clock every Monday two of the workers' wives would help to do the weekly wash – 'that happened every Monday right through my childhood and beyond,' says Aubrey.

'There was also a great big baking oven in our kitchen where every Tuesday bread was baked. Always Tuesday. Three faggots were pushed into the seven-foot-long brick oven, then set alight. When the embers were

*Elmley Castle below Bredon Hill, Worcestershire.*   73

*Flatford Mill pool with Willy Lott's cottage, Suffolk, – the setting for John Constable's celebrated painting 'The Hay Wain'.*

glowing red hot, about twenty big lumps of dough were placed above the embers, using a long-handled shovel called a baker's peel. Then the steel door was closed to keep in the heat. Twenty minutes later, the dough would be baked into lovely crusty cottage loaves. The smell was wonderful, and we boys often were given a still-hot slice to eat. You didn't need butter or jam when the bread was fresh from the oven like that and when it was made from home grown wheat, milled between huge millstones at the Southwater windmill, and later, at Warnham water driven corn mill.

'My mother looked after all the baking, and some yeast was saved to mature for the following week's bake. Several of the labourers were given loaves as part of their wages.'

Wednesday was always butter-making day. Aubrey's mother had been trained in this art before she was married, so she was an expert, churning the cream into butter in what was called an end-over-end churn. Making butter usually took about two hours with the churn turning – which was very tiring – shared between the woman of the house or one of the maids and a farm worker or gardener brought in specially to help.

'But by the time the dairy equipment had been scrubbed and packed away another day had gone, which is why different days were allocated to the different major tasks around the house. Thus Thursday was ironing day, and Friday general shopping day.'

Of course farms were almost completely self-sufficient until well into the twentieth century, growing their own animal and human feedstuffs and killing their own animals. Aubrey remembered pigs being killed now and then in the yard and the process of preserving them.

'The belly parts were salted down in a huge chest that we called the brine tub. About sixty pounds of salt was used for the belly pork from one pig. The salt stopped it going bad. Belly pork was a luxury for the farm workers when they came into tea, at hay-making time.

'There's a funny story connected with pork that I ought to tell you. My wife and I were sitting in the dining room one day in 1966 when a great big piece of soot crashed down the chimney and onto the dining room floor. My wife picked it up and threw it out the window into the garden – then later that same day we saw the dog was licking at the soot so we went to investigate. And would you believe it – that piece of soot turned out to be a great big piece of bacon that had

been hung to smoke up the chimney at least twenty years earlier by my father – probably just after the war. We cleaned the sooty meat and ate it – it was delicious!'

Smoke from the huge fire was a really useful preservative – Aubrey remembered long strings of home-made sausages: 'Hanging on hooks close to the ceiling along the beams, they sometimes lasted for months before they were finally used up yet they never seemed to go bad.'

At New House Farm eight farm workers sat at the table at five o'clock when the hay-making was in full swing. They had home-made bread and cold belly pork, home-made cheese and butter, washed down with home-made cider. Only half an hour was allowed for this meal, as all hay was pitched by hand and the faster the work was done the better – any delay, and rain might spoil everything.

Deep in Norfolk, Will Constance remembered a similar round of household chores, but he also recalled the pressure to conform in a countryside still deeply conservative.

'Mother baked once a week on a Friday and washed on a Monday. That was the way all women did it then, and if a woman didn't do it like that on those days she was considered beyond the pale – she'd be virtually ostracised! I suppose it was all part of the fact that in every area of life there was a way to do things and it was strictly adhered to. Any deviation was frowned on.'

And if the routine around the house was strictly regulated other areas of life were – by modern standards – rather lax. Throughout the fens a preparation called Daffy's Elixir was hugely popular. Easily and cheaply bought from chemists it was in fact a laudanum preparation – a form of liquid opium – that was perfectly legal and designed to be given to children to keep them happy and quiet! By all accounts it was highly effective and there were similar opium-based preparations that could be bought without prescription for adults. But in those days health was a difficult matter to deal with in remote rural areas. Will Constance remembered some of the hardships.

'I had four brothers and three sisters who all died in infancy. Most families had lost little children – disease was everywhere, particularly TB and smallpox, and of course if you had no money you could not get a doctor even if you were dying. My father ran four miles for the doctor soon after one sister was born and the doctor brought my father back with him in the pony cart.

*Dawn on a winter river.*

'I think old people had the worst of it when I was a young man. I've lived into the age of social security, but if they had no one to look after them in the old days they starved or froze to death. Neighbours might help, but they could easily end in the workhouse and many would rather die in a ditch than that.

'It wasn't easy for women either, particularly if they had husbands who spent all their wages in the pub. And many did, while their wives struggled to bring up twelve or thirteen children in a tiny cottage without heat or light or water as they are known today.

'Everything was different then, every detail. If you could go back in time the first thing you would notice is that everyone wore drab clothes, black or brown or some other almost nondescript colour. All the women wore ankle-length dresses when I was a boy and leather, button-up boots. The men always wore hob-nailed boots made of the thickest leather.'

But if life was hard from a health point of view there was still fun to be had with one's friends, as Reg Dobson recalled from his youth on a Shropshire farm.

'I shared a bed with my friend who was also called Reg when I finished school and started working full-time on the farm. I'd hear my friend shout "Wake up Sam!" I'd leap out of bed in a panic and he'd immediately leap into the warm place I'd made in the bed. We were both called Reg, but for some reason we called each other Sam all the time. Lord knows why. We used to share the same bed and the room had two windows which we kept open winter and summer, however hard the weather. Some mornings the pot under the bed would be frozen over it got so cold.

'We lived in a farmhouse like every other farmhouse round about – a house with no electricity, no gas, no heating other than big old fires, no easy lighting and no labour-saving devices at all.

'We had oil lamps for light and everything had to be scrubbed clean without detergents and washing powders. It was all brute force really, and elbow grease. My wife and I had two children, both girls, and Gladice had read that fresh air was good for babies so we left them out for a couple of hours every day, even when a gale was blowing, but it did them no harm!'

Far off in the West Country Joe White spent most of his life in a long, gaunt-looking stone farmhouse – a typical Devon longhouse where traditionally the family lived at one end, the animals at the other and the two ends were divided by a corridor that ran through the middle of the house from front to back. Joe's longhouse is older than anyone seems able to guess. Certainly it was there when the compilers of *The Domesday Book* approached the local lord to ask for a list of his farms and servants, freemen and villeins. But even then it was almost certainly an ancient house.

If you took any group of farmers alive in the last decades of the twentieth century, Joe would probably stick out as someone whose life had changed least since he began farming before the Second World War. He had never been to London and rarely left the confines of Devon. When he was interviewed in the 1980s – already then well into his eighth decade – he was still doing his best to be self-sufficient: his vegetable patch was his pride and joy – neat rows of onions, potatoes, leeks, cabbages and beans were tended with great care while all about the farmyard chickens wandered happily, providing eggs and meat.

'Like a lot of old boys round here I used to grow a lot of my vegetables for competitions at the Chagford Show. They gave prizes for the biggest onions, the biggest leeks

*Wiltshire. A quiet corner of Lacock village.* 77

78    *Buckland-in-the-Moor, a tiny village just off the slopes of Dartmoor.*

and carrots, but I liked it mostly for the talk and the argument. It's a sociable thing.'

And like so many older farmers Joe had nothing but contempt for the European Union.

'I've never gone away from here because the world's gone mad – I'd get in the way with my old ideas, but I can't help thinking they're better ideas. Take my cows. I have names for the cows not bliddy numbers which is what the EU is all about.'

Down on the Weald of Kent Lance Whitehead's old farmhouse has hardly been touched in four centuries. It's a perfect example of a timber-framed medieval hall-house converted during Tudor times to a house with two floors; but other than that, it has hardly been altered in three hundred years. Of great historic interest now, it was originally just a yeoman farmer's house of no great pretensions. It has no damp course and the baked floor tiles in the sitting room are laid straight on to sand.

'Well the floors do sweat a bit in winter I must admit,' said Lance. 'And rain comes down the chimney, but it's warm enough so long as we burn a couple of wheelbarrow loads of logs each day!'

Until the passion for all things new reached absurd heights in the 1960s and 70s relatively few ancient farmhouses had been demolished, but those two ill-fated decades destroyed a sizeable chunk of the historic countryside – and many of the demolitions are now deeply regretted. Occasionally of course there was nothing for it but to re-build – in the days before timber preservatives and woodworm treatments old farmhouses could seem almost to crumble back into the soil from which they had originally come, as Richard Body remembered.

*A fine ancient timber-framed market hall in Essex.*

79

80    *Dorset. Milton Abbas church and houses under snow.*

'When we moved to Hope Farm it was an old wooden house that had sunk and subsided till it was incredibly crooked – the floor from one side of the bedroom to the other went down by about six inches – can you imagine that – all the furniture was constantly in danger of falling over. The problem was the age of the house, the marshy ground and the fact that really old houses had almost no foundations.

'Downstairs it had hammered earth floors – it got so bad with vermin running about in it that one year a rat stole my father's teeth!

'Hope or Jemmet Farm as it was called was probably built in the mid 1500s, but we pulled it down in the 1960s – in 1967 to be precise – it was beyond repair.'

Small family farms once littered the countryside and those who owned or tenanted them rarely saw themselves as a cut above the rest – the sons and daughters of smaller farmers had to be up working when the maids and farmhands arrived for work and effectively they all mucked in together.

But the gentleman farmer was a very different figure. He might have an in-hand farm and several other farms that were tenanted and provided him with a rental income. Such farmers tended then, as now, to send their children to public schools and to live a life very different from their poorer neighbours.

Blundell Williams is a good example and when he was interviewed in the 1990s he recalled, for example, how the better off, gentleman farmer was able to afford his own carriage.

'Yes, when I was a boy we had a number of different kinds of carriages. The phaeton, I recall, was a rather grand thing. It had four wheels – unlike the dogcart or the Gamboge which both had two – and it was pulled by two fine horses. It was a very comfortable, sprung affair which would easily carry four people in great style and comfort.

'The dogcart could also carry four. It had two seats in front and the underlings – the groom or one's children – sat on a sort of box affair at the back. Below this was a

*Milton Abbas, Dorset. The village had sixty-one thatched cottages with two hundred inhabitants. Mrs Jacobs mows the grass in front of her cottage.* 81

*Young vixen at the mouth of her earth.*

82   *A quiet Essex lane, late 1950s.*

*Children found ways to travel that were not entirely dissimilar to their parents' carriages and carts.*

board on which you rested your feet. None of the roads in this remote part of north Wales were metalled then as you can imagine and we were often cut off in winter by drifting snow – but when the valley flooded, when I was a young man, even the carriages were hopeless so we used to go by sailing boat to Denbigh to the hunt balls.

'Long after the electricity came we still had to resort to lamps and candles in winter when something went wrong and although we were isolated here there was always plenty to do – we had lots of friends to go and see, we visited each other's houses, and there was hill

hunting, tennis and rough shooting. And of course as a child one could be mischievous and invent one's own pastimes. I used to get up to lots of pranks. I remember once as the maid was serving us at dinner – the whole family had sat down – I produced a live slow worm out of my pocket and a great pile of plates crashed to the ground from the maid's hands. I was reprimanded rather severely for that.

'In my youth it was still the custom in many if not most country houses to say morning prayers in the house. The head of the household, one's father, would

lead the prayers. One morning during prayers I found it difficult to take it at all seriously because I noticed that our terrier was taking a great interest in a big old cupboard in the corner of the room, what we called a Jonah cupboard. As soon as I could I opened the cupboard door and spotted a big rat. I prodded him, he leapt and our terrier caught him in mid-air. That I'm afraid was of far more interest to me than the prayers on which I should have been concentrating.

'I suppose like all children I used to do some pretty mad things – I was terribly fond of chickens I remember, but I couldn't afford any fancy poultry, which I loved, so I used to buy ordinary chickens and paint their legs bright colours!

'On a farm you never know what you may have to do – I remember my wife coming back from a hunt ball in a rather lovely dress and then, still in the same dress, she had to feed our pigs. We had about thirty sows then, but we never really made any money with them.

'We had a car quite early on – an old Austin that lasted for twenty-three years. Then we had a Morris 8, but we had to get rid of that because the nanny grew too fat to get in it! We thought nothing of travelling long distances by carriage in the days before the motor car. We used to have a cook, two maids and a nanny, but those days are long gone. The nanny, who lived in, was paid £16 a year.'

Like many smarter country house farms, Blundell's Glynn Arthur had an inside loo by the turn of the twentieth century, but it was reserved strictly for use by the women of the house. The men still had to go outside and they continued to do so until long after the First World War. The staff had another, entirely separate loo, which was also outside.

Yorkshire farmer John Elgey remembered the cavernous gloom of farmhouses before electric lighting, and the faint glow of dim oil lamps. The oil lamps that lit the house were not terribly efficient – 'they cast a poor yellow light and made shadows everywhere' said John – so there were several attempts to find a better do-it-yourself system.

'We rigged up acetylene gas lamps. These lamps were fitted to the walls of the rooms and had lead pipes running to them. The lead piping went to an old outhouse where we kept a special generator. You had to fill this with carbide which came in big drums in the

OPPOSITE: *Stanton village in the Cotswolds, Gloucestershire.*

*Lynmouth, Devon, where the East and West Rivers reach the bay.*

form of what looked like big stones. You put the carbide – the stones – into a trough which then slid into a big tube in the generator. Then you carefully screwed home a gas-tight door. Then you set the thing going and water dripped onto the carbide inside the generator which caused the gas to come off. The vessel in which the gas was released was like a barrel floating in a bigger barrel of water and, as the gas built up, the floating barrel rose higher in the water and then gradually sank as you used up the gas. When it had all gone the lights went out and you started all over again. But if they went out in the middle of one of mother's parties we'd use paraffin or get out the old oil lamps again!'

Lance Whitehead's Forstall Farm, high on the Weald of Kent, started life in the late 1400s, but then it was just a massive draughty hall with the smoke curling out through a hole in the roof.

'There is some ancient blackening on the roof timbers, but it is believed that when the house was first built they didn't even have a hole in the roof. They just hoped the smoke would gradually work its way through the thatch as, of course, it would. I suppose although it would have been cold the fact that the roof was then so high – as there was no first floor – meant that the smoke would have billowed around and gathered well above the heads of the people down on the ground. The chimneys were probably put in when the first floor was built, perhaps one hundred years after the hall was built.'

The massive oak staircase has treads made from solid carved triangular pieces of oak and across the ancient creaking ceilings corridors and narrow passages lead through rooms that seem to double back on themselves. There is hardly a straight wall to be found anywhere, but the massive wall and roof beams have survived the centuries and if all goes well Forstall Farm is likely to look out over the Kentish Weald for many centuries yet.

*Gloucestershire. Ancient cottages at Arlington Row, Bibury.*

88   *An Essex wheelwright at work.*

# 5.
# COUNTRY CRAFTS

The twentieth century saw more changes in the way we live than any previous single century. From a world where energy was provided either by the horse or by steam power, we have moved to a world where we have tapped the vast resources of nuclear power; we have explored the outer reaches of our solar system; we can fly across the world in enormous comfort in less than a day and we routinely employ computers and telecommunication systems of staggering complexity.

In the midst of these momentous technological changes it is easy to forget how many ancient crafts survived long into the twentieth century in remote corners of the countryside.

In the Forest of Dean, Gerald Haynes, the last free miner, was still at work in the 1950s and 60s; Eustace Rogers was still making coracles on the Severn at Ironbridge as his ancestors had made them three centuries earlier; Jack Durden was still making charcoal deep in a Gloucestershire woodland in a tradition dating back to Roman times.

And then there were the wheelwrights, the rake and hurdle makers, the harness men and the trug makers – many were still with us well into the second half of the twentieth century when John Tarlton photographed so many dying trades.

John Piper is a good example. He was still making wagons and wagon wheels in Kent until long after the Second World War. Like so many craftsmen, John took his own skills for granted but anyone who saw him carve the fellows (part of a wooden wheel) and then make each spoke fit into it perfectly would have been astonished at his technical virtuosity for this was craftsmanship of the highest order. However, having carved and fitted the timber section of the wheel a critical point was reached: the point when the iron cart-wheel rim had to be fitted to the outside of the wooden rim.

The trick was to heat the iron rim in the forge until it was red hot. It would then be forced onto a newly made wheel. The heat would make the metal expand, but even then it would still be a tight fit and would have to be hammered on to the wooden rim of the new wheel – from there it is easy to imagine how tightly it gripped the wheel when five or six buckets of cold water were immediately thrown over it and it shrank round the wheel. Cartwheels were so tight and well made they might run for fifty years with perhaps just two changes of rim in all that time.

Using local produce – whether timber for wheels or leather from local tanneries – was once the rule rather than the exception in the countryside and self-sufficiency in everything was an economic necessity. The result was a range of clever homespun solutions to various problems and needs.

Bee-keeping is a case in point. It was very popular in times past in many rural areas – with shops sometimes miles away and sweet goods expensive, the prospect of a ready supply of honey was an alluring one. And hives were not always those wooden miniature houses we see today – country people used bee skeps woven from straw by the bee skep man.

*Fog in the country. In the late afternoon in this Cotswold beechwood the fog rises up among the trees.*

Wheat straw was the best straw for skeps. It was mixed with bramble and hazel to keep the straw together and then built up pretty much as straw mats are built up. A bee skep was a simple, hollow basket without all the internal arrangements that a modern wooden hive has.

Traditionally a bee skep would have a hackle on top – a sort of straw hat – to keep the weather off, and it would rest on a stone slab. Under these circumstances a skep might easily last a century or more.

It is a little easier to check inside a modern hive, but bees were just as happy in straw if for no other reason than straw is a wonderful insulator: a six-inch thick piece of wood has the same insulating power, for example, as one inch of straw.

In deep woodland areas often well away from even the smallest hamlets another very different trade was a feature of the traditional countryside for here the charcoal burner plied his lonely calling.

Before the Industrial Revolution, in the days when the Weald of Kent was one of the great industrial areas of Britain, charcoal was a vital ingredient in the manufacture of iron. The important thing about charcoal for the old ironmasters was that it burned at very high temperatures relative to wood and thus made iron smelting possible. Canon for the Tudor and Elizabethan warships that sailed across the world were made in these areas because the abundance of hardwood meant plentiful supplies of charcoal.

To supply the ironmasters, large numbers of men were involved in the charcoal-burning business, but the history books have little to say about these shadowy figures who worked in remote locations and constantly moved about the country. But if we know little about the charcoal burners themselves we do at least know something of the techniques they used to turn timber into charcoal. The main reason for this is that charcoal-burning never really did entirely die out in Britain. Though it has not been used in iron smelting for nearly two centuries charcoal still had its uses until the 1960s and 70s: until synthetic products made it redundant it made an excellent filter for a number of important industrial processes and was also used to make artists' materials.

*An itinerant knife grinder, a craft still common in the early 1960s when this picture was probably taken.* 91

92    *Millstone dresser at work: the grooves had to be re-cut regularly to allow the grain and bran to escape after milling.*

Jack Durden, who was born in 1925 and was still working in the 1980s, was one of the last of the traditional charcoal burners. He enjoyed a curious nomadic existence, constantly moving about the country from his native Dorset up through Wiltshire and Gloucestershire to the high beechwoods of Buckinghamshire. A lot of old woods had been neglected before and during the war and forestry owners were happy to get Jack to come along and use up the mass of timber that the trade wouldn't take.

'The point is that you don't need a specific kind of timber to make charcoal,' he remembered. 'Almost anything will do, although of course if you were able to choose you'd always go for a hardwood. Beech is absolutely ideal and oak probably the next choice. Soft wood doesn't last as long and gives less heat, and as it's lighter it produces less charcoal. Since we sold it by weight, using soft wood meant we earned less money.'

Originally charcoal burners worked by digging pits in which the burning took place, but this was labour intensive given that, by its very nature, the charcoal burner had to move frequently to follow the tree fellers.

The mobile kiln was ideal because it was light enough to carry. It came in two sections each about six feet in diameter, but the top about four feet high and the bottom about three feet.

'With charcoal-burning the real skill comes in loading the kiln, especially the bottom half. You have to load it so the wood creates a channel for the air from the air inlets to the smoke outlets.'

'The bottom of the kiln contained four smoke outlets and four smoke inlets – 'they were just holes really,' said Jack, 'but the wood had to be carefully stacked so there was a narrow gap from inlet to outlet. On top of the stacked wood we'd then place plenty of what we call black wood – that's wood that hasn't quite become charcoal from a previous burning.

'In the top three foot section of the kiln we'd stack more four-foot lengths – again like a box of matches if you can imagine that – and then we put the lid on. Now if you imagine that the bottom section is four foot high with four-foot lengths of wood arranged vertically that's fine. But the three-foot section also has four-foot long pieces of wood in it arranged vertically – this means that the total height of the stacked wood is eight feet where the height of the kiln totals seven feet. This is very important because when you put the lid on you want about a foot of wood sticking up above the top of the kiln itself. You put the lid on the wood and then light the black wood, which is now in the centre of the kiln, with an oily rag.

'With the four air inlets and the internal channel you get a tremendous draught and the fire will burn fiercely. It's a chimney on fire really. Then the wood sticking out the top will gradually sink and settle. The lid will then go down and rest properly on top of the kiln. You then seal round the lid with sand. It has to be a really good seal for the thing to work properly. The sudden lack of air in the kiln is what starts the carbonising process – the process that turns the wood into charcoal. People think charcoal is just slowly burned wood – it isn't. It's wood that's been carbonised at high temperatures.

'Once the lid's tightly on, there's no more through-draught and the heat can't escape so it goes back down into the stack of wood. The heat builds up even more and then just when the smoke turns blue – it takes experience to know precisely the right moment – you seal all the inlets and outlets at the bottom of the kiln. The whole thing is then left sealed for roughly forty-eight hours. If it is not properly sealed the wood will all burn away and you'll have no charcoal. If all goes well your two-and-a-half tons of wood will have produced seven hundredweight of charcoal.

'The marvellous thing about charcoal-burning was that you got to live and work in beautiful remote locations away from noise and other people.'

Charcoal-burning provided a living for hundreds, if not thousands, at one time and it had the added advantage of helping to use up wood that might otherwise have been wasted.

Another natural resource that was once vital in the countryside was clay – it was used to make the ubiquitous clay pipe which was found in almost every country district until long after the end of the First World War. When tobacco arrived on these shores during the reign of Elizabeth I a flourishing pipe-making industry quickly grew up. Such was the popularity of a weed which was then believed to be positively beneficial.

The very first pipes – made when tobacco was ruinously expensive – were carefully crafted from solid silver but these are now extremely rare. As the habit of smoking took hold and the price of tobacco went down cheaper pipes made from clay began to appear. Clay pipes utterly dominated the scene for over two centuries but by the middle of the ninteenth century cigarettes and briar pipes were gradually being introduced – cigarette popularity increasing dramatically during the Crimean War – and slowly but surely the clay pipe began to be superseded.

In the heyday of clay some three thousand makers were involved in the trade but by the early years of the twentieth century things had changed drastically, although one or two clay-pipe makers survived until the Second World War and beyond.

We may no longer approve of smoking – it is, after all, terribly unhealthy – but for good or ill some smokers still insist that clay produces a more satisfying smoke than any other material.

The technique for making clay pipes was fairly simple. The wet clay was rolled roughly into the shape of the pipe and then left to cool for a day: a fine metal rod was then passed up the stem and left in position. The pipe was placed in a mould and then in a press known as a gin. A lever on the gin was pulled to make the final, carefully moulded shape, complete with bowl. When the piercing rod was removed from the stem, any rough edges were smoothed off by hand and the pipe was left to dry. The final process was firing the pipe in a kiln. After firing, the stem ends were coated with wax or lacquer – an old practice designed to prevent the smoker's lips sticking to the clay.

Kiln firing, whether for pipes or bread ovens or for brick-making, relied on a plentiful supply of wood – and this didn't just mean heavy logs. The harvest of timber produced by the coppicer fuelled the ovens and provided the raw materials for a number of trades.

Coppicing, the art of harvesting woodland by periodic cutting to ground level, has been carried out since ancient times. It was still practised well into the twentieth century and has recently enjoyed a revival. Bill Hogarth was still working as a coppicer in the 1960s.

'I've been coppicing for fifty years and more,' he said during an interview given towards the end of his working life. 'I started straight from school with my father during the last war. His father – my grandfather – had been in forestry too. Coppicing was a reserved occupation during the war because the government needed thousands of ship's fenders and they needed us to supply them. For the first ten years or so we used axes to cut the trees, but then the early chain saws came in.

'As well as the saw, we also used a special peeler – like a chisel with a bevelled end – to strip bark. I used to

*Arthur Torode was seventy-six when this picture was taken. He'd been a blacksmith for sixty-one years.*

work through about fifteen acres of wood a year. In the depths of winter I'd make besom brooms from birch cut during the early winter. Birch is used for the brush part and the handle is hazel.

'When you coppice a wood, every last part of a tree is used: young hazel, for example, has many uses – for bean poles, fencing, walking sticks and, of course, for brooms. Then there's oak. The bark from young oak trees is taken off and the resin it yields is used for an essential part of the leather-tanning process. Even the roots were used – they were very popular with florists for flower-arranging bases!'

Coppicing was always a cyclical affair. Hazel was cut every six to seven years, birch anywhere between eight and sixteen; the oak cycle was every twenty-five years and alder, ash and sycamore anywhere between fifteen and twenty-five years.

The demise of coppicing changed the look of the countryside but a countryside without a horse harness and collar maker in every district would have been inconceivable to our grandparents. Today the men who kept the horses working have all but vanished.

Terry Davies was still making collars in the 1970s and 80s – one of the very last men in the country to do so. He explained the nature of the work.

'It's a full-time job making maybe thirty-five collars a year and the same number, perhaps slightly fewer, sets of harness. I was trained as a saddler, but got more interested in collars and heavy working horses generally. After my apprenticeship I worked with an old man who'd made collars when working horses could be found on every farm in the country.

'The point is that a horse collar is like a hand-made pair of shoes. You can't rush it and each collar is made exactly to the measurements of a particular horse. No collar will fit two different horses although a well-made collar will outlive the horse and its owner!

'Once you've got your measurements – a shire horse will vary between twenty-five and twenty-seven inches – you make the pipe or forewell as it's known, that runs

*'Riddling' out the cut hazel. Only the best rods were kept for hurdles while others were used for props and pea-sticks.*

*An old Somerset industry. Tying hair for use by the brush-makers.*

*Testing whey for acidity was an essential part of small-scale cheesemaking.*

Hawk', 'barking irons' and 'fromard', while the main aid to hurdle-making was a vice called a brake.

Willow and ash were the timbers used. Willow was lighter but not as long-lasting as ash and it took longer to make because the willow had to be barked first.

The secret of a good hurdle was always said to be that you should 'leave enough room for the shepherd's foot' between the upright and the diagonal brace. Traditionally this was essential so the shepherd could push the hurdle into the ground using just his foot.

In the early 1960s hurdle makers were still common, but within a decade and with the arrival of metal pens they'd all but vanished.

But what about those wonderful-sounding tools? Well, the Tommy Hawk was an old-fashioned device for making mortises – the joint used to attach the rails to the end pieces. The barking iron was like a chisel with a sharp-edged fifty-pence piece stuck on the end. It was used, as the name suggests, to strip the bark off the timber.

The fromard was an extraordinary tool. It was like a big metal L. The short arm went into the wood and the long arm was used as a lever to split or cleave the wood. All the rails were split rather than sawn. When you split wood it follows the grain round the knots and other imperfections and the wood retains its strength. Sawing cuts through the fibres and weakens the wood.

The brake was like a primitive vice that lifted and gripped quickly so the hurdle maker could move the wood around as he worked on it. A good hurdle that was kept well covered when not in use would last a generation.

From archaeological evidence we know a great deal about the timber products of the past. We know, for example, that some two thousand years ago pole lathes were being used in England to cut and turn bracelets from shale. To this day in Egypt and other third world countries pole lathes exist that are in essentials identical to those used in Britain for a thousand years.

In Britain the real home of the pole lathe was the area around High Wycombe in Buckinghamshire where English chairs were traditionally made. Here vast areas of beechwood – the staple of the chair-making industry – had always been available to the chair and pole lathers whose numbers increased dramatically as the nineteenth century progressed.

round the front of the collar. This is a leather tube about four inches in circumference and it's stuffed like the collar itself with hay. Next you stuff the collar proper with straw. The collar itself is sewn together using conventional saddlery techniques, but what you have to remember about a collar is that although it's part of the harness it's also separate in that it exists only to give the horse something to push against. It's really just a cushion, but vital to the whole operation.'

For driving ponies a collar would be completely leather-lined but for a big working horse wool is the chosen material. Leather would make the horse sweat whereas wool absorbs sweat. And of course wool was usually locally available – a fact that was once central to the whole idea of manufacturing.

Wooden sheep hurdles were – and to some extent still are – part of sheep farming. But when most lambing was still outside on the hills hurdles were absolutely vital.

A traditional craftsman could produce six hurdles a day using tools that had wonderful names like 'Tommy

*Alfred Sparrowhawk assembles a willow hurdle in his workshop near Oxford. Light yet strong, willow hurdles were a vital tool for the sheepfarmer.*

*West Country
lobster-pot maker.*

The vast increase in the urban population living in small houses created a huge demand for cheap wooden chairs and High Wycombe and other similar areas expanded to meet the demand.

The chair bodger was the man who made the turned parts of the chair – the spindles for the back, the legs and the cross pieces. Bodgers in the High Wycombe area rarely made the seat or completed the whole chair, but a related tradition in Herefordshire and other rural districts saw craftsmen turning their hands to seats, poles, backs, spindles and assembly – the whole thing in fact.

It was the Arts and Crafts movement at the end of the nineteenth century – a reaction against the machine-made age and in favour of craftsmanship – that delayed the demise of the pole-lathe men and helped keep the craft going into the 1950s.

It is difficult to describe exactly how a pole lathe works, although to see one in action is to realise it is simplicity itself. A springy sapling is fixed in the ground and attached – at the thin end, which should be above the worker's head – via a cord to a lathe. When the lathe operator pushes his foot down on a pedal the cord is pulled, the pole bends down and the lathe turns. When

*Frederick Clayton, the clock and watchmaker of Puckeridge, Hertfordshire, took over his father's business in the 1920s and ran it for sixty years. Here in his workshop he is repairing a bracket clock.*

the pressure is released from the pedal the springiness of the pole turns the lathe in the other direction by pulling upwards. All the while the craftsman's various chisels are cutting and shaping the turning wood.

Apart from the pole lathe the chair makers and bodgers used an adze – a medieval tool that was traditionally used to scoop out the shapings in the chair seat. The rule was always: the better the seat, the bigger and deeper the scoops.

Traditionally pole-lathing was winter work – chair bodgers did other things in summer.

When farm implements were all made locally and from local materials, enormous ingenuity was often required to make a serviceable tool from limited resources. But this often produced a situation where, over centuries, tools developed that were so well-suited to the task in hand that they have never been superseded even by tools made with the latest hi-tech materials.

A case in point is the hay rake. It might seem that a metal rake would work better and last longer, but in fact wooden rakes – made in exactly the same way for centuries – are more comfortable and efficient to use than modern metal ones. Traditional wooden hay rakes are now very rare indeed but at least one man was still making them into the 1990s.

In the tiny hamlet of Dufton near Appleby in Cumberland, the Rudd family had been making wooden hay rakes for over a century. They made some 14,000 rakes a year, but as late as the 1970s still used the tools and techniques that were used when the business began in 1892.

Hay rakes were made from three timbers – ash, pitch pine and silver birch. The ash and pine were used to make the head and shaft of the rake respectively. The sixteen teeth were always made from silver birch. Traditionally pitch pine was used for the handles and a rake handle was a standard six feet long.

So how were rakes made? First the six-foot-long shaft was shaped. Next a small wooden ash hoop about half an inch in diameter, softened by boiling for ten minutes and then shaped into a semi-circle, was used to hold the head onto the shaft – as it dried out and hardened, the hoop gripped like a vice. A traditional rake involved the use of just four nails – three in the hoop and one into the shaft.

Birch was used to make the teeth because it was plentiful and hard wearing – essential since the teeth did all the work. With care a rake would last twenty years – testimony to the strength of a tradition of manufacture that had lasted well because it worked.

Equally efficient yet even more ancient was – and is – the practice of thatching houses and among thatching materials reed reigns supreme. In terms of insulation and longevity it is still as good as most of the modern alternatives. Reed-cutting was the trade that supplied the thatchers with their raw materials and it is one of the few country crafts that has experienced something of a revival in recent years.

'It's the best roofing thatch there is,' says Eric Edwards, one of the last of the Norfolk reed cutters. Sixty years ago vast areas of Norfolk's wetlands produced a rich annual crop of reed that was sent to thatchers all over the country. Then thatch began to be replaced by tiles and slates and the old reed cutters gradually died out. When Eric started on the Turf Fen Marshes near Ludham in the 1960s, the craft of reed-cutting was already in decline, although plenty of the old hands were still around to pass on their skills.

100    *Country gunmaker at work on a new stock.*

*The slow process of turning a tree into planks in the saw-pit.*

'There's actually more demand for reed now than there was when I started as a young man,' he said. 'The point is that during the 1980s and early 1990s people began to realise that the countryside would lose much of its charm without a few thatched houses. New people learned the old trade of thatching and it became something of a boom industry. I think people also realised that thatch was actually a very good roofing material. It's very warm – a superb insulator – and Norfolk reed thatch will last as much as eighty years.

'Most reed is cut mechanically, but there is a real skill in mowing reed – that is cutting it with a scythe. I made my own scythes – you have to since you can't buy them any more because no one makes them. I used to work my way along a dyke, find an alder growing naturally with the right sort of bend, cut it, and add some handles. A scythe is still much better than the mechanical cutter when the water is high so it wasn't just sentiment that kept me doing it the old way. I'm also proud of the fact that I was one of the few – possibly the last of the cutters who knew how to mow reed by hand in this way.

*Thatching is one of the very few old trades that has experienced a genuine revival.*

103

'The only other tool we used was the rake – not like a garden rake but a long pole with three nails in it. The rake was used to clean the reed – that is strip off any roots and bits of side shoots. We call this dressing the reed. It's really just cleaning it up but it was a most important thing because if reed isn't cleaned after you've cut it you can't get it into neat bundles.'

Norfolk reed was cut from mid-December until 5 April but that didn't mean Eric was out cutting every day right through the winter – far from it, in fact.

'Well, the great difficulty was that reed needs water and lots of it, but if there's too much water you can't cut it because you can't get into the marsh. We had a system of sluices that could help keep the water levels where we wanted them, but if there was too much rain even the sluices failed to help. We needed a good easterly wind – that used to drive the water out.'

In an average season Eric would cut something between four and six thousand bundles.

'We didn't sell reed by the ton or the yard – we sold it by the bundle. That's the way it's always been done. A bundle used to be what the old boys described as "tied by a fathom". That meant you got five or six bunches of reed and when you stacked them upright you could tie them round with a piece of string measured at six feet long. For me these days a bundle is just what I can get my arm round.'

Most of Eric's thatch was sold locally despite the temptation of cheaper foreign imports. 'Well, I had my favourite customers and I didn't like to disappoint them!'

Norfolk reed varies in length between four feet and perhaps six or seven feet and the best bit, as Eric explained, is the bit at the bottom.

'You see, that's the fat or butt end. It's the end that's always been in water so it's the strongest. It's the bit you will see when you look at a thatched roof. The higher, tapering part of each bit of reed will not be visible.'

Eric's marsh covered more than three hundred acres on both sides of the River Ant about halfway between Yarmouth and Norwich. He lived where he worked, too, and loved the fact that when he was at work he could always see his house in the distance.

In addition to reed he cut sedge which was used for ridging work and both reed and sedge were cut on a two-year cycle.

'That's a lot better for the wildlife. Less disturbance you see, and there's a lot of wildlife wherever there is

*A quarryman splitting slate by hand at Llanberis Quarry in Wales.*

reed. I regularly saw bitterns and otters for example. Both, I think, are making a bit of a comeback. But being able to work in a place where you see so much wildlife was part of the appeal.'

Once the reed was bundled up Eric carried it out to a specially prepared area where dry chaff, or shucks, had been laid to provide a dry base.

'You never tie wet reed or stack it on wet ground – that's the golden rule. We stacked the bundles about ten high so that the wind could get into them. We'd come along later with the boat to take the whole lot off the marsh. Yes, it was a wonderful life. Keeps you fit and in touch with nature, but people now want a different life; not out alone on the marsh.'

*Hampshire. Cutting withies on the Avon water meadows. The six to eight feet long shoots were harvested each year.*  105

106    *Making lobster pots from withies grown in the Avon watermeadows. Fisherman at Mudeford, Hampshire.*

Like thatch, trugs have never quite died out though they are far more difficult to obtain now than they were before plastics and cheap imports made them seem unnecessarily expensive. The word trug comes from the Anglo-Saxon word *trog* meaning a wooden vessel, trough or boat and though trugs have been made in Britain for centuries they only really came to the attention of the public after the Great Exhibition of 1851. While visiting the exhibition Queen Victoria bought several trugs displayed by Thomas Smith, one of the great Sussex trugmakers. Smith was so pleased that he apparently took the Queen's trugs to London himself, in a wheelbarrow!

Once it was known that Victoria was using trugs they went from being a practical item used by country people to something of a fashion item. Gardeners all over the country started to use them and the trug-making industry blossomed in Sussex. Directly and indirectly trug-making provided thousands of jobs in the Herstmonceux area of Sussex – which had always been the centre of the trug-making industry – for the next century or more.

Then in the 1960s came disaster: trug-making nearly died as plastics made wooden buckets, bowls and baskets a thing of the past. Only a handful of traditional trug makers survived the really hard times, but survive they did and in recent times there has been a resurgence of interest in this ancient art. True there are a number of manufacturers who use plywood to mass-produce trugs that have a vaguely traditional look about them, but the old sweet chestnut and willow trug can still be found.

The old Sussex trug came in sizes numbered one to ten. The smallest – the No. 1 – measured just seven inches long and had a capacity of one pint; the biggest – at one bushel – was thirty inches long and could carry a sack of potatoes.

Between size seven and size eight there was a distinct change in the way in which a trug was made. Up to size seven a trug had feet made from willow; at size eight and above trugs were made with chestnut straps – two forming a V-shape running underneath.

The old trug makers claimed that the real work was in the preparation. Putting the thing together took ten minutes. The skill was cleaving and shaping the various pieces of wood before the trug was assembled. The main tools used in trug-making were a drawknife, a horse (a sort of foot-operated vice), an axe for cleaving and hammer and nails.

Willow was used for the trug boards – the flat slats from which the body of the trug was made – and sweet chestnut for the hoops and handles. Trug-making probably developed in Sussex precisely because there was an abundance of chestnut and willow.

After the willow was cut and shaped into boards it was soaked in a barrel of rainwater for half an hour or so. The chestnut for the hoops and handles was cut in winter and brought straight into the workshop to be cleaved – that is split rather than cut. This helped it keep its strength – vital because it was the hoop that kept the trug together.

The chestnut hoop was steamed and shaped around a block before being nailed. With the hoop ready the boards were nailed into place. The widest board was nailed into place first to make the bottom or keel of the trug. After that the other boards were gradually nailed on, getting narrower as they went up the sides.

The great thing about a trug was that as it got older it got tighter and stronger – a good trug might easily last sixty years.

Despite the lack of hi-tech materials many rural technologies were specifically built to last. For thousands of years, until steam and later electricity, grain – for example – was milled using ancient wind- or water-powered systems. And of course the miller was central to the rural community because bread was a staple.

Just one working water-mill survives today on the Thames but it is a fine example of something that was once common across the British countryside.

The huge ancient wooden mill wheel at Mapledurham in Berkshire, still turns. Inside the mill, equally ancient wooden walls creak and groan – particularly when milling is in progress – as the building moves and settles. Like most ancient wooden buildings Mapledurham Watermill is held together almost entirely by wooden pegs and joints.

Throughout the mill are signs of the past – an old blackened candle holder, scratched figures on the grain-dressing machine, worn boards where generations of millers have turned in the same places on the wooden stairs. One miller has even carved his initials on the desk beside the window which faces upstream – here no doubt generations of millers sat and watched the barges bringing grain or carrying flour away. At Mapledurham grain is milled as it would have been milled at the time of Domesday. But despite its antiquity, Mapledurham is

*Blades being replaced on the watermill at Coggeshall, Essex.*

a commercial set-up selling top quality flour to local shops, farmers and bakers.

*The Domesday Book* records that 'William de Warene holds Mapledurham of the King...there is a mill worth twenty shillings'. But even before William the Conqueror's great survey we know that there was a mill on the site because the Saxon chroniclers mention it.

Much of the fabric of the present building dates from the fifteenth century when the mill served communities on either side of the Thames. Like most long-established businesses it has known prosperous and near disastrous periods over the years. During the early 1660s, for example, the fact that the Plague raged in London brought the mill great prosperity, for the royal court – and that would have meant thousands of courtiers and attendants – moved from London to nearby Abingdon. Huge amounts of flour for the people and bran for their

animals would have been supplied. And as London expanded in the eighteenth and nineteenth centuries the mill continued to do well using barges to send its produce downstream to the capital.

By the beginning of the twentieth century cheaper wheat flour from America and Canada spelled the end for the traditional British mill, whether wind- or water-powered. Hard Canadian wheat needed large electrically-powered mills in place of stone-ground milling. By 1920 the 10,000 or more working wind- and water-mills in England were reduced to less than two hundred. On the Thames, where once there had been a mill every mile, they vanished – all, that is, except Mapledurham which struggled on supplying flour and bran for local estate farms. By 1940 even Mapledurham could no longer compete and the mill closed. But sheer good luck prevented it being converted into a house or demolished. True it fell into a bad state of repair, but never quite so bad that it could not be brought back to life.

After being used as a film set in the 1970s, the mill earned enough money to pay for its own restoration – and that is precisely what happened. By 1977 it was back in operation as a fully commercial business.

The mill produces about a ton of flour a day – a tiny quantity compared to a big industrial flour mill, but what the flour lacks in quantity it certainly makes up for in quality. The slow speed of the mill stones compared to electrically driven stones, keeps the natural oils in the flour.

The four-and-a-half-foot diameter millstones at Mapledurham are French in origin and are extremely hard. They will last for upwards of fifty years, but they need to as they are very expensive to replace. The stones are cut or dressed in two ways: the main furrows and the tiny chisel-cuts, or stitching, in the flat areas between the larger grooves. This is where the fine grinding takes place and it has to be done with great precision because you need ten or twelve cuts to the inch.

Every part of Britain would once have had one or more mills but if mills were ubiquitous so too was basket-making or weaving – and perhaps the most useful of all the trees in the countryside as far as basket-making is concerned is the willow. A fast-growing tree that is easily propagated, the willow could be used for everything from baskets and tools to eel catchers and cricket bats. Perhaps the greatest centre of willow growing and harvesting was Somerset.

*Up to the 1950s and 60s huge medieval barns were still used to store farm produce. This magnificent example is at Cressing Temple in Essex.* 109

*The bookbinder at work on a leather binding.*

*Norman Nash, from Hamworthy, Dorset, at work replacing lead on the cupola of the church at Blandford Forum.*

Right across the Somerset Levels and beyond, willows were always grown in vast profusion to provide the raw material for thousands of basket weavers and hurdle makers. In the 1920s and 30s, eighty per cent of the population in the area was said to be involved in willow-growing, basket-making or hurdle-making.

The blackmole willow was one of the most popular varieties. Harvested once a year and at any time between October and the end of March the cut pieces were three to five feet long; Somerset hurdles were typically six feet long and various heights – up to about seven feet.

Having been cut the willow wands were stacked and then boiled for two hours to make them pliable. A completed woven hurdle would last perhaps a decade or more. Willow baskets of every conceivable type and size (including those designed to trap eels and salmon) kept thousands of workers in employment.

112    *Headkeeper, Fred Thurgood of Terling, Essex, stops for lunch with his labrador.*

# 6.
# SPORTS AND PASTIMES

Country people have always been suspicious of change. Given the cycle of the growing year, mistakes were too expensive to be tolerated – mess up a harvest and you have a full year to wait for the next. And the truth is that for most of the time the old ways generally worked well, or at least well enough to ensure that local communities could survive. They might often be close to the borderline of real poverty – occasionally families or whole villages would cross that line – but generally the traditional ways kept life going.

And if there was a reluctance to change the cycle of the farming year there was an equal reluctance to give up the old entertainments that the countryside had relied on. Even in the 1950s most rural communities, unless close to a big town, were too far from cinemas and theatres for them to be a regular source of entertainment – which is why the village pub still held sway as the chief source of the countryman's entertainment.

Half a century ago virtually every village and hamlet in the land, however small, would have boasted a pub. A huge number of these have now gone. Until the late 1950s when John Tarlton took so many of his pictures they were still rather ordinary places – they really were public houses in the sense that they offered a fire, a few chairs and served drink, but that was the full extent of it. Very few served food and most were rarely visited by anyone other than locals. With no one-armed bandits or juke boxes country pubs were quiet places where beer was simply poured from barrels; what's more the beer was still produced locally and fizzy lagers and fancy foreign cocktails were unheard of.

Norfolk farmer Will Constance insisted that pubs changed little between his young manhood in the 1920s and 30s and the 1950s and early 1960s.

'I'd get a lift into Diss sometimes at weekends to whist drives and dances so we had some fun but we mostly went to the pub. But I always remembered my father's warning that pubs were for man's use not for man's abuse. Pubs were dingy old places in those days before the Second World War, full of smoke and with bare stone or brick floors, rough wooden chairs and benches – and not a woman in sight. Women wouldn't go near a pub then because if a woman went in a pub on her own it was assumed automatically that she was a prostitute. There were no exceptions to that.'

There's no doubt that the pub was an important place of relaxation for country people and Will's recollections of the atmosphere of the pubs he knew is remarkably vivid.

'Every pub looked the same more or less when you went in. A big fire, a few scrubbed deal tables, dark low ceilings and a few old boys sitting round with their mugs of beer and smoking hard – everyone smoked short clay pipes for all they were worth. When you went in a pub you couldn't see through the smoke some days – and people think cigarettes are bad! Mind you, with a few candles or an oil lamp the only light it wasn't surprising you could see so little! Besides, there was nothing much to see in most pubs. People were there to drink and play cards or dominoes. Things were very different then. Just you imagine – you go in the pub and the first thing the landlord does is give you a pipe. That's what used to happen when he knew the man.

113

*Country postman.*

'They would go from pub to pub. I remember one old boy, Tom Reeve, who would have been fifty or sixty when I was a boy. He used to drink in the King's Head in Scole after tying his pony and cart up outside. Well, one day it ran off and we all watched him tearing down the road after it. We had a good laugh over that.'

Apart from dominoes and draughts, which were always popular, there was another pub game that dominated many rural districts and it is a game that has now all but vanished: quoits.

Will Constance recalls the heady days when quoits were all the rage.

'Quoits matches were always being played in every pub yard. A quoit is a ring of iron weighing as much as eleven pounds. There was an iron peg with a feather stuck in it that was driven into the centre of what we used to call the quoit bed. It was a clay area that was designed to make the quoits slow down or stick a bit.

'No money was ever bet, but a gallon or two of beer might go to the winner of a game and the loser then bought the beer. You had to throw your quoits eighteen yards and each man had two quoits. Four men would play at any one time. The last place I saw it played was at Billingford Common in the 1950s. Like horses, it just seemed to reach the end of its days and it disappeared almost overnight, but the older generation of men loved it all over Norfolk. I suppose the men who'd played it had played it since they were young and they still enjoyed it, but as they died out their sons had other interests – motorbikes and cars.'

Then there were the ploughing matches which attracted men from miles round about.

'We used to go on Saturdays to the drawing matches. I won a lot of prizes at this. Prizes were usually given by local tradespeople and the first prize was nearly always a copper kettle. Other prizes would be tools of one sort or another. On a Saturday we might walk as far as eight or ten miles to get to a match. At a drawing match the horses and ploughs were already there, and you'd just draw – by which we meant plough – one furrow. For ploughing matches you had to plough with your own team and you had to do a certain minimum number of furrows, perhaps twelve or twenty. It was all judged on how level your ploughing was. Bad ploughing is very easy to spot, but there wasn't much of that where we were because the ploughmen who entered the matches really knew their stuff.

'My father hated a new pipe so when the landlord gave him a new one he'd straightaway give it to another old boy till it had been smoked black, then my father would have it back. He liked 'em well worn in as he used to say. Improved the flavour of the smoke.'

Many of the pub regulars were farmers and agricultural dealers there to strike a bargain over a glass and a pipe, and this was particularly true on busy market-days when many of the pubs did a roaring trade. On other days the pub bar might remain almost empty for, as Will says, 'there were very few visitors, no tourists or holidaymakers.' It was local men or nothing, but on market-day the men would make a big thing of the pubs.

*A quiet smoke in a country pub.* 115

'In the last days of horse-ploughing the men would drive round in cars to take part in the different matches – they could clean up on the prizes – and then suddenly it was all over for ever and there were no more horses and no more ploughing.'

In summer the village boys would fish in the ponds. Most of these were destroyed in the 1950s and 60s as roads were widened and improved to take the seemingly endless increase in the numbers of cars and lorries.

The ponds were a great source of fun for village children. A thick hazel wand from a hedgerow would be cut to make a fishing rod but bent pins would not be used as hooks. Real hooks made all the difference so they were begged, borrowed or bought and looked after like gold, and the technique for fishing was entirely different from techniques employed today when cheap, almost invisible nylon lines have turned a gentle pastime into a competitive sport. A strong thread – thinner than the sort used for tying parcels but probably at least a millimetre thick was used as the main line

116   *An Essex lane near Hatfield Peverel.*

*Evening on the flooded watermeadows at Christchurch in Hampshire.*

with a couple of feet of catgut tied for the last stretch before the hook. Today nylon line is so cheap that gossamer thin line can be used throughout, but as late as the 1950s tackle was still largely a home-made affair. So the hook would be tied to the gut – or occasionally to two or three hairs taken from a horse's tail and woven together – and long summer days would pass catching roach and rudd, bream and gudgeon. When a fish was caught there was no thought of throwing it back alive which is the common practice today – it would be taken home and either eaten or given to the cat. Among the wealthier sections of rural society in upland areas fishing – of a very different kind – was also popular. Fine cane rods by London makers and reels by Hardy would be used to catch trout and sometimes salmon from local streams and rivers. The old social divide between those who fished for coarse fish – the labouring classes – and those who fished for trout and salmon – the landowners and bigger farmers – was still strong.

Shooting of course was also hugely popular among the better off. Formal shoots would be organised with teams of beaters and perhaps a dozen guns all of whom would be old friends. Having enjoyed a day at one house the same group of friends might move on the following Wednesday or Saturday to the next formal shoot and so on through the season.

Hunting was the other great rural pastime and although it latterly became far more egalitarian it was largely a pastime for the wealthy in the middle decades of the twentieth century, though of course spectators would have come from all classes and the professional huntsmen might be local farmers.

But away from more formal pleasures like hunting, shooting and fishing there were the pleasures of simply working, playing and of course drinking together. Football of a rather primitive sort was also popular, as Reg Dobson recalled from his early Shropshire days. 'When we killed a pig, one of the best things was that we were able to use its bladder – with a bit of effort – to make a really good football. You just blew it up and tied a knot in it and it lasted for ages.'

Reg also remembered that betting was hugely popular, but in rural Shropshire in the 1940s and 50s it had little to do with formal sports like racing, as he explained.

'We adored betting on silly things – on whether a man could drink ten pints in ten minutes, for example, or if he could ride a particularly difficult horse. Betting always reminds me of Bubber. He was a wild old boy.

He was a real giant of a man who once took a bet in the Lamb at Drayton that he could drink ten pints while the clock struck ten. The landlord said he'd have them drawn and on the counter at the appointed hour. At about nine o'clock Bubber went out of the Lamb which was unusual for him – under normal circumstances he'd never leave before closing time. No one knew where he'd gone, but at five minutes to ten he was back. When the clock struck, up went the first pint and the other nine followed in quick succession. After he'd collected his winnings the man who'd bet him said:

"Why did you go out at nine o'clock?"

"To see if I could do it, of course!" said Bubber. "It's no use betting if you don't win."

The pub was very much the centre of social life in Reg's youth and men would walk every evening to drink at their favourite local which could be five or six miles away from some of the more remote cottages and farms. The pub gave men their only chance to escape the drudgery of everyday life. For the price of a few drinks they could enjoy a temporary escape into a world of laughter and good fellowship. Reg Dobson again:

'One night we were chatting in the Lamb about various subjects – dogs, horses, bets and so on – when Bubber said he could eat five-dozen eggs. We immediately bet him a pint a-piece that he could not. After the pub shut we all trooped across the road to the fish and chip shop. Mr Weston, the owner, fried five dozen eggs and Bubber ate the lot with the greatest of ease. We paid up.

'Talking about Bubber reminds me that we used to have horseback tug-o-wars with teams from the various farms and big houses competing. We had one once at the big house where Colonel Donaldson Hudson lived – he was the local squire. He entered a team as did the surrounding farms. We got to the final and had to pull against the colonel's team.

'As we got going and took up the strain, one of our horses started misbehaving so father put his coat over her head to calm her, but that made her worse and she reared. Bubber slipped off her – everyone was riding bareback – but we still held our own. Then, seizing his chance Bubber leapt back on, gave an almighty heave and all the colonel's men and horses were pulled over. We'd won but we were disqualified because you had to let the colonel's team win. That was the way they thought in those days. The squire couldn't be seen to be beaten by men who in many cases worked for him.

*A frosty day on the Hampshire Avon.* 119

120    *Country pubs were once the most important source of entertainment in rural areas.*

'We used to get our own back on him, though, by laying trails of raisins the day before he was to have a big shoot – the raisins, which pheasants love, led to our wood and away from his! As a result we had plenty of pheasants.

'Eating competitions, like the ones I've already mentioned, were a big thing in my youth in Shropshire and I believe this was true of many other country districts. I suppose it was good, simple entertainment when we had little else.

'The wagoner on a farm near us was a phenomenal eater. People used to come and fetch him to eat for bets. One night a farmer knocked at his door and asked his wife if he would come and eat a whole calf for a bet. She wasn't in the least surprised by the request. She just said she didn't know if he'd do it because he'd already gone out to eat two ducks down at the Fox for a bet.

'"I'll go down there and ask him," said the man. He found Bill, put the proposition to him and Bill, having eaten his ducks, went off straight away and ate the calf as well!'

In East Anglia the shallow, flooded fields and meres provided a different kind of entertainment. Using animal bones tied to thick leather boots the young men of Suffolk, Norfolk and Lincolnshire made perfectly good skates and looked forward intensely to days of hard frost. In fact East Anglia produced all Britain's champion skaters in the first half of the twentieth century, but skating was also popular in Kent and elsewhere. Kentish farmer Aubrey Charman remembered skating on the his local ponds.

'We always skated on the pond in front of the house in winter for weeks on end, but sometimes we'd go further afield for the challenge of different waters. But by the late 1960s winters were never quite cold enough and the ice was never thick enough. We used to skate late into the evening when the moon – or as we called it the parish lantern – was out. There is an exception to that general run of warmer winters, however – 1963. That was a terrible winter but it meant we had our fill of winter sports!'

Church attendance was high in rural districts between the wars and for many the reason had less to do with religious fervour than with the simple love of singing and good company. Bell-ringing was popular for the same reason.

Aubrey Charman had records of his family's comings and goings as far back as 1749, but these only begin to include substantial details in the middle decades of the nineteenth century. Aubrey's great-grandfather, for example, was the first warden of the village church, which was built in 1850. He sang in the same church choir for seventy years and Aubrey himself sang there every Sunday for fifty-two years before stepping down in favour of his son.

For Devon farmer Jo White the local market, rather than the local church, was a huge source of pleasure – he made money there selling his produce but also had the chance to catch up on friendships with other farmers round about.

'Farming used to a be a sociable thing – we'd meet at the shows and have a great gossip and we'd all press our apples and have cider at harvest time when we went round all the farms helping each other. They were times of such pleasure I will never forget. My brother would come round and my friends and we'd all help each other and we'd drink and talk in the fields. They were happy times. What laughs we had and good old chats about everything.

'We even used to help the fat major with his ploughing too – he had one of the farms nearby and we liked him though he was an incomer. I had two brothers and a sister and we all worked then, and I can remember the fun we had in the cornfield at harvest time as the last bit of it was cut and the rabbits came pouring out. They were everywhere, dozens of them, hundreds sometimes. The dogs used to chase them and the children – everyone! There are fewer rabbits now – old myxy has seen to that – and we have less corn. But rabbit-catching days at harvest time or with the ferrets were memorable happy days.'

For Lance Whitehead on the Kentish Weald, shooting was a passion, as it was and still is for many farmers and other country people.

'We used to have great rabbit-shooting days before myxomatosis – it was never as it was in Edwardian days on the grand shoots where they'd say about a duck or a pheasant "Up goes a guinea, bang goes a penny and down comes half a crown!" We just used to get together with all the farmers round about for vermin shoots – you know rabbits, jays, magpies and so on – and it was our bit of fun and way of socialising because it's very difficult for a farmer to take a holiday as you can imagine. I did try it once or twice but it doesn't work well. You have to get someone in to do the work and he won't know your animals, won't know what each

121

122    *Exmoor. Badgworthy Water near Cloud Farm, just above Malmsmead.*

animal is fed, when and how. So you have to give him a list of what needs doing and it's all very hit and miss. You worry when you're away and you have to sort it all out when you get back. Much better to stay at home and enjoy the traditional pastimes and socialising of country people.'

One of the greatest changes in the countryside was the coming of the wireless, as the radio was known when it first became available to all but the very poor in the 1920s and 30s. In the evenings country people would gather around the one wireless in the village and listen astonished as crackling across the airwaves came the sound of concerts in London or the voice of the prime minister. Compared to TV and radio today it was all primitive in the extreme but to country people who had grown up through the long silences of an earlier period, with only letters and newspapers to connect them to the outside world, the wireless was little short of miraculous.

It wasn't until he was well into his teens that Cleveland farmer William Wade heard his first wireless. He can still remember the sense of disbelief as the weak sound crackled over the crystal set.

'It was like magic – you just couldn't believe it. At

*End of the day: shooting was always popular in country districts.* 123

124   *Roach fishing in a lake near Tewkesbury, Gloucestershire.*

that time we'd only heard talk of radios and of course television wasn't even an idea. That cat's whisker set I first heard wasn't even ours. One of our farm workers had it. The sound was a bit faint but it was very exciting. The only other entertainment the modern world had brought us was the cinema – every now and then we'd traipse off to the pictures in Stockton or Darlington to see the silent films. People would travel miles to see them in those days.'

For William radios were only slightly more entertaining than the local horse-fair – he wouldn't have missed that for anything.

'Going to the horse-fair was one of the highlights of the year. I remember going to the one at Yarm – it was always held in September and I loved it. After meeting old friends and catching up with the news there was always serious business to be attended to – I remember being sent to Yarm to buy a pony to run the milk. I found a pony I liked and asked the man holding it if it had ever been in the shafts. It had, so I asked what he wanted for it. Forty pounds he said so I offered £30 and we settled on £35. That bargain was quickly made but it wasn't always like that – haggling for what seemed like hours over a pony wasn't unusual and could be great fun if exhausting!'

For the better off, a riding pony or horse was as essential as a car is today. In north Wales, Rowley Williams' earliest memories are of riding various ponies.

*A Scottish gillie with his ponies.*   125

*Farringdon church in Hampshire where Gilbert White (1720-1793), author of* A Naural History of Selborne, *used to preach.*

'I loved horses and ponies and in my memory I always feel I spent my whole childhood on horseback. I rode from the time I was a very small boy; it was unthinkable then for a boy, or indeed a girl, not to learn to ride. It was how we got about and, of course, you couldn't hunt if you didn't ride and all our friends and neighbours hunted. Hunting lay at the heart of all our social activities. I was perhaps three or four years old when I learned to ride and I was still riding in my seventies. I was joint master of the Flint and Denbigh hounds for more than fifty years and my son took over from me. So hunting, like farming, is very much in the family. I was very keen on hunting from an early age, it was just so exciting and central to our whole social life because all our friends did it.'

One of the curious things about the Rowley Williamses is that, like many country people with a great love of hunting foxes, they were also very fond of them and over the years kept several as pets.

'We had one for a number of years when I was young and I remember if I shouted "Come on Charlie!" he would rush over and jump into my arms, but eventually every fox will wander away. I think the mating and travelling urge is just too strong and they eventually have to go. Much as I loved him poor Charlie was bound to disappear eventually and he did – one morning I got up and called him and he was gone. Other foxes we kept used to wander around the house and sleep with the dogs. One used to play with the hounds – the fox would hide in the shrubbery in the garden while the hound puppies tried to find it. They'd draw for him in the undergrowth while he sat, with a rather superior look on his face, bang in the middle of the lawn!'

House parties, hunt balls and weekends at each other's houses were also central to the life of the Rowley Williamses and their circle.

'We had lots of friends to go and see; we visited each other's houses, and there was hill hunting, tennis and rough shooting. And, of course, as a child one could be mischievous and invent one's own pastimes – climbing trees, races around the fields, hunting for birds' nests and of course fishing.'

Travel for the sheer pleasure of seeing new places was a completely foreign concept in most country districts until well into the 1960s, as John Elgey explained.

'Certainly people never worried about travel whether locally or further afield. The first bus came to this part

*Evening rise on Loch Ailsh, Sutherland.*   127

of Yorkshire in about 1925 – before that everyone walked everywhere unless they had a cart or a wagon or could get a lift on one. But people very rarely went anywhere outside their immediate locality. There was nothing to go to unless you had to travel for work or go on some specific business – in fact people thought it was an expensive or time-consuming nuisance if they had to go somewhere. The idea of travel for pleasure was beyond most people.

'But that first bus was a pretty sight. It had a beautifully made wooden and brass body which could be lifted right off the iron chassis. So when the man who ran it needed to cart pigs and sheep he manouvered the bus under a beam in his barn and used a block and tackle to lift up the wooden coach body. Then he'd leave that hanging there and lower a different wooden body on to the chassis. In this he could cart animals or people.'

The church seems to have played a lesser part in the life of the countryside in the early part of the last century than one might imagine, but where it had a strong influence individual priests were often heartily disliked. Reg Dobson's memories of country parsons perhaps typify the two ends of the spectrum; on the one hand the parson who was a friend of the community and on the other, the parson who wasn't afraid to let it be known that he felt he was far superior to his flock.

'I was very fond of one parson we had when we were in Shropshire. He used to play in the village cricket team in which I also played. He used to say that there were only two things he was any good at: cricket and preaching. I remember he used to say – "I became a parson because I could preach and I knew it would also give me more time than any other job to play cricket." Yes, he was a great man, but I remember another parson of a very different kind. I won't tell you his name, but he was a real bad lot. Treated all the kids like dirt and we hated him. He put me off parsons for life.'

*Ancient wooden pattens on the wall of the church at Walpole St Peter, Norfolk.*